PROPHECY AND ETHICS

Isaiah and the Ethical Traditions of Israel

ERYL W. DAVIES

Journal for the Study of the Old Testament
Supplement Series, 16

Sheffield
1981

BS
1515.2
.D3
1981

Copyright © 1981 JSOT Press
ISSN 0309-0787
ISBN 0 905774 26 4 (hardback)

Published by
JSOT Press
Department of Biblical Studies
The University of Sheffield
Sheffield S10 2T N
England

Printed in Great Britain by Redwood Burn,
Trowbridge and Esher
1981

British Library Cataloguing in Publication Data

Davies, Eryl W.
    Prophecy and ethics. - (Journal for the study
    of the Old Testament Supplement series; 16)
    I. Title   II. Series
    224'.1'06   BS1515.2

    ISBN 0-905774-26-4

CONTENTS

PREFACE

This book is based on a thesis entitled Prophecy and Ethics: An Examination of Ethical Traditions as Reflected in the Oracles of Isaiah which was submitted to the University of Cambridge for the degree of Ph.D. in 1978. The body of the thesis remains largely unchanged, but in preparing the work for a wider readership I have omitted a lengthy excursus on the Hebrew levirate marriage, since this was tangential to the main theme of the present volume. Exigencies of space have made it necessary to give the references which appear in the footnotes in an abbreviated form, but a bibliography of all the works referred to may be found at the end of the book (pp.153-172). Chapter and verse enumeration follow those of the Massoretic text, for which Biblia Hebraica Stuttgartensia (1967-77) has been used. The biblical passages quoted have been translated direct from the Hebrew, but so far as possible the wording of the Revised Standard Version has been followed.

I wish to register my special debt to my supervisor, Dr. R.E. Clements, both for his generous help, guidance and encouragement at all times, and also for extending his personal kindness to me during my period as his research student. I wish also to express my gratitude to numerous friends for reading parts of the original thesis at various stages of its preparation, and for redeeming it from both errors of judgement and infelicities of style. Special thanks are due to the editors of the Journal for the Study of the Old Testament for their helpful comments and suggestions, and for their kindness in including this work in their Supplement Series. I am deeply grateful to the managers of the Bethune-Baker and Hort Memorial Funds for the generous grants to assist in its publication.

The book is dedicated to my parents for their continued interest in the work and for their constant support and encouragement.

Eryl W. Davies   November, 1980
Department of Biblical Studies
University College of North Wales
Bangor

7

INTRODUCTION

Few attempts have been made in recent years to analyse in a systematic way the ethics of the Old Testament, especially as it relates to the teaching of the eighth-century prophets. In general, the subject of ethics has been regarded simply as a subsidiary part of the broader study of biblical theology, and it is perhaps significant that during the past forty years only two major monographs have appeared which deal explicitly with problems concerning the ethics of the Old Testament /1/. The present study represents an attempt to analyse, in so far as possible, the basis of the ethics presupposed in the oracles of the prophet Isaiah. The investigation was carried out because it was felt that although questions of morality are at the very centre of Isaiah's message, this remains one aspect of the prophet's teaching which has not received the attention it deserves.

This study will be primarily concerned with the presence and use of traditional themes and motifs in the preaching of the prophet. The method adopted will be a form-critical analysis of certain passages in Isaiah the authenticity of which have not generally been disputed. One difficulty which attends any examination of prophetic oracles is the possibility of diverse interpretations of the same passage, and consequently these various interpretations must be given due consideration before any attempt is made to analyse the ethical rationale underlying the prophet's indictments.

The whole question of the relation of the prophets to tradition has, of course, been the subject of much scholarly debate, and the earlier tendency to emphasise the "new" or "creative" element in the prophetic preaching has by now largely given way to the notion that the prophets are to be understood in relation to the ancient traditions of Israel, especially those of the covenant and the law. Indeed, it is argued that much in the prophetic literature of the eighth century B.C. gains in meaning once it is realised that the strictures of the prophets are based on the presupposition that Israel was bound to Yahweh in a covenant-relationship. Since this relationship was expressed in and maintained by the law, the indictments of the prophets were thought to have been

9

occasioned by a neglect on the part of the people to comply with Yahweh's expressed will. It has further been argued that the form and ideology of the divine covenant in Israel was based on the pattern of the treaties between the suzerain and his vassal which were prevalent in the ancient Near East, and it is thought that the prophets of Israel were influenced in their language and imagery by certain ideas and expressions which recur in these political treaties.

It is clear, therefore, that any attempt to examine the assumptions which have been thought to underlie Isaiah's ethical pronouncements must take into account the possibility of a background in the covenant or in the vassal-treaty upon which this covenant is thought to have been based. Moreover, since the law was an expression of Yahweh's will for the covenantal community, it will be necessary to discuss passages where appeals to the law have been found or where legal provisions might conceivably be in question. In addition, we shall examine the possibility that Isaiah's oracles were influenced by ideas and expressions prevalent in wisdom-circles and, further, the assertion that his proclamations of judgement were based on the teaching of his contemporary, Amos, will be taken into consideration.

The opening verses of Isaiah (Is. 1:2-3) will provide a convenient starting-point for the present study, since these words have been regarded as indicating influence from the sphere of the wise in addition to influence from the realm of covenant and treaty. The passages discussed in the third and fourth chapters will have as their theme the notion of "social justice", and here also the possibility of the influence of tradition on the thought of the prophet will be examined. It will be argued in these two chapters that the social problem as viewed by Isaiah resolved itself for the most part into a question of land-ownership. The economic system in Israel and Judah during the eighth century B.C. was based largely on agriculture, and some of the most heinous offences against which the prophets inveighed occurred in connection with property. Owing to its paramount economic importance, land was the way to wealth and it is not surprising, therefore, that it should have become the chief object of acquisition. It will further be argued that Isaiah's concern for the maintenance of justice "in the gate" is not unrelated to his accusations against those who dispossess the poor of their patrimony, since the right to speak in the legal assembly was contingent upon the

10

possession of property. The purpose of the introductory chapter is to place the present study in its proper perspective by surveying the research which has been carried out on the subject of the ethics of the prophets since the days of Wellhausen and Duhm.

Chapter One
PROPHECY AND TRADITION

PART I: Survey of Past Research

It will be convenient to begin our outline of recent research on the subject of the ethics of the prophets with the contributions of Wellhausen and Duhm, although it should be emphasised at the outset that the views which these scholars expressed were not entirely new or unprecedented. Their work can, however, be taken as representative of the critical approach to the prophetic literature which prevailed towards the end of the nineteenth century.

The determinative factor which influenced the views of these scholars concerning the ethical contributions of the prophets was undoubtedly their recognition of the fact that Israel's faith had progressed from the crude, tribal religion of the Mosaic period to a glorious climax in the teaching of Amos and his contemporaries. The acceptance of the Grafian hypothesis provided an important turning-point in this regard, for the source of the Pentateuch which had hitherto been recognised as the oldest came to be regarded as the most recent, and this naturally engendered a drastic change in the picture of the whole development of Israel's religious history. Wellhausen himself placed the Decalogue of Ex. 20 in the time of Manasseh, and regarded it as a product of the prophetic school of thought /1/. The relation between Israel and Yahweh in the period of Moses was that of a natural bond which was only later replaced by a relationship based on conditions of a moral character /2/. Indeed, it was only with the eighth-century prophets that a sense of awareness of the ethical dimensions of the relation between Yahweh and Israel began to emerge, and consequently these prophets came to be regarded as primarily ethical and moral reformers whose teaching represented the culmination of the religious development of Israel. Wellhausen's dictum that the law was in fact later than the prophets meant that these men could no longer be regarded as interpreters of a legal tradition originating in the time of Moses; on the contrary, they were to be regarded as great innovators and as the pioneers of ethical monotheism /3/.

In this way, great emphasis came to be placed on the creative contribution of the eighth-century prophets, and they immediately assumed a far greater significance than had hitherto been attributed to them. Since the teaching of these prophets could no longer be regarded as having a basis in tradition, it was assumed that they spoke with the authority of inspiration /4/. Consequently, it was important to realise the nature of the power that seized these men before any attempt could be made to comprehend their teaching. It is not surprising, therefore, that much emphasis was placed on the capacity of the prophet to receive the word of God and to respond to it accordingly, for it was the message which he had received in such moments of divine inspiration that he was called upon to proclaim to his contemporaries. God had revealed himself to the prophets in the depths of their heart and they became conscious of him as the source of the moral requirements demanded of men. Their moral concern was, therefore, the outcome of a profound religious experience which belonged to the highest category of spiritual insight, and the true significance of the prophets lay in the fact that they were in the privileged position of being able to discern the true character and nature of Yahweh. They conceived of God as possessing certain moral features, and they believed that this provided a norm of morality which should be reflected in man's actions towards his fellow-men. Thus Isaiah at the time of his call encountered the holy God in the sanctuary (Is. 6:3), and this encounter determined his entire preaching and the way in which he was to interpret Yahweh's demands. Isaiah, therefore, placed before the people the standard of divine holiness, and his task was to fashion the internal order of Judah in conformity with the holy character of God. The evils which were prevalent in Judah resulted from the fact that the people had ignored the commanding presence of the holy God in their midst /5/.

The personal experiences of the prophets were therefore regarded as of paramount importance, for it was through such experiences that the prophets were able to grasp certain truths about the nature of God and his requirements of his people. The ethical values which they embraced were regarded as having been directly inspired by God himself, and it was believed that the task which these prophets were called upon to fulfil was simply to explicate the nature of Yahweh's being and to emphasise that the fundamental object of worship was that men should become like him. Mercy and compassion were among the features which the prophets regarded as the essence of Yahweh's being, and they believed that those who revered God would have to exhibit in their everyday actions those qualities which inhered in him. Thus justice, truth and mercy were not simply abstract concepts but constituents of God's own character. This was why the prophets entertained such a lofty idea of Yahweh's demands and why they constantly extolled the sublimity of his moral claims. Men must judge their conduct by no lower standard than the absolute goodness of God, and their actions must always be measured against this transcendent ideal. Yahweh was a just God and all injustice must, by implication, be an offence against him. In this way, the nature of sin was defined by the nature of the deity sinned against. Thus the message which the prophets proclaimed and the standard of conduct which they demanded of the people evolved quite naturally from their overwhelming apprehension of God's character.

The ability of the prophets to discern the true nature of their God and the fact that they were believed to be attuned to the secrets of the divine counsel gave them a unique significance and invested their teaching with a special importance. Indeed, as a result of the elevated position which was accorded the canonical prophets, they were distinguished sharply by many scholars from the large number of other prophets whose activity was only indirectly related in the Old Testament. According to Duhm, Amos' reply to Amaziah the priest to the effect that he was no prophet nor the son of a prophet (Am. 7:14) was significant in this regard, for Amos was, in effect, distinguishing himself from his ecstatic predecessors and contemporaries who represented the lower and more primitive levels of prophecy /6/. These prophets would normally have regarded themselves as being isolated from other men by virtue of their ability to induce ecstasy and to utter oracles while in the possession of the divine spirit. Indeed, it was this ecstatic experience which ensured that the prophets' credibility would not be impugned. Amos, on the other hand, appeared in Bethel with no credentials other than the word of Yahweh, and in stressing the fact that he was merely a shepherd and dresser of sycamore trees (Am. 7:14) he was emphasising that he was simply an ordinary citizen engaged in a similar type of occupation to that of his hearers. He was therefore not a prophet of the "professional" type whom Amaziah was accustomed to meet, for he was not susceptible to ecstatic experiences of the wild, orgiastic kind normally associated with such prophets. Yet, it was precisely because he was simply an ordinary shepherd and nevertheless able to speak Yahweh's word that Amos' position was invested with a unique status, for he was, in effect, making the appearance of the true servant of Yahweh contingent upon a special commission and not upon any outward manifestation of ecstasy or possession of special gifts. Amos could lay claim to a direct intuition of divine truth and to an immediate revelation of Yahweh and he therefore felt no need to authenticate his mission by showing himself to be in a state of ecstasy. It was primarily for this reason that Amos and the other canonical prophets marked a radical break with the contemporary prophets who regarded their profession as a trade and whose utterances were the result of their ecstatic experiences. Thus, according to Duhm, the new element which emerged with the eighth-century prophets was a manifestation of spiritual power which brought them to an altogether different plane of religious insight, and this was the factor that gave to classical prophecy its unique and abiding significance.

Some scholars, however, were conscious of the danger of distortion and oversimplification in such a view of the prophets, and it was felt that Duhm and his contemporaries had placed far too much emphasis on the mystical receptivity and spiritual perception of these men. It came to be recognised that comparatively little could be known about the personal religion of the individual prophets and it was emphasised that they themselves did not appear to have conceived their task as being to witness to what they had experienced in their relation to Yahweh. The primary factor was the message which they proclaimed and the impending judgement which they announced as the inevitable consequence of sin. This approach undoubtedly provided a welcome corrective to the views of Wellhausen and Duhm who had regarded the prophets primarily as theologians rather than as bearers of Yahweh's message.

Many scholars, in fact, came to recognise that this message could only be comprehended adequately if due account was taken of the sociological conditions out of which the prophetic message arose. A proper understanding of the nature and form of the society which the prophets knew was the essential prerequisite for any assessment of the import of their message, since their preaching was related in a very direct way to the contemporary social scene. This approach, exemplified in particular in the works of Weber /7/ and Causse /8/, marked a shift in emphasis from the prophetic figures themselves and the psychology of their inspiration to the intense involvement of the prophets in human affairs and their reaction to the concrete, social situation of their day. But while these studies were helpful in emphasising that the pre-exilic prophets could not be understood without considering the political, economic and sociological conditions of their times, they suffered somewhat from onesidedness in that they regarded the prophets simply as the champions of the oppressed and as the advocates of new ideas of equality and freedom.

Despite this new approach, however, the pioneering works of Wellhausen and Duhm continued to give rise to much scholarly debate concerning prophetic consciousness and the psychology of prophetic inspiration. Hölscher, in particular, sought to analyse the abnormal experiences of the prophets whose actions and utterances are recorded in the Old Testament, and he concluded that even the classical prophets were ecstatic, though not quite in the same sense as the earlier prophets whose ecstasy was induced through music and dancing and whose utterances were completely unintelligible /9/. In examining the words of the classical prophets, Hölscher made constant reference to the earlier type of prophecy and to reports about dervishes and visionaries from different ages, and by equating phenomena which were in practice separated by several centuries, he tried to construct a unified picture of the nature of biblical prophecy. Similarly, T.H. Robinson argued that prophecy was characterised above all by its ecstatic nature, and even the utterances of Amos and Isaiah were thought by him to have resulted from their ecstatic experiences /10/. Unlike Duhm, he maintained that it was the prophet's ecstatic experience that provided the guarantee of Yahweh's presence and message, and he suggested that the boldness of Amos' words to Amaziah could only be explained on the assumption that the prophet was protected by the superstition which held ecstasy to be sacrosanct /11/. Further, Abraham Heschel argued that the fundamental element in prophecy was a communion with the divine consciousness and a sympathy with the divine pathos, although at the same time he expressed grave doubts concerning the ecstatic element in Hebrew prophecy /12/.

As research advanced in the sphere of Israelite history and religion, it became increasingly clear that a fundamental reassessment was necessary of the position of the prophets in the religious development of Israel. Wellhausen's view of the growth of religion from rudimentary beginnings to an advanced monotheism was gradually being discarded, for scholars came to realise that such a neat, evolutionary scheme did less than justice to the element of progression and regression which were such characteristic features of many periods in Israel's religious history. Moreover, it was recognised that the law as enshrined in the Decalogue and the Covenant Code could be traced back to a comparatively early period in Israel's history and it could not, therefore, have been dependent upon the teaching of the prophets.

The major work in this field was done by Albrecht Alt who sought, on the basis of form-critical analysis, to discover something of the pre-literary history of Israelite law /13/. He distinguished between casuistic law which was used in the normal secular legal procedure and which contained many parallels with the laws of the ancient Near East, and the apodictic law which represented the pre-Settlement religious law of Israel. However, Alt's general conclusions concerning the origin of apodictic law in the cult have been seriously challenged /14/ and his assertion that this law was uniquely Israelite must be abandoned in view of the parallels found in extra-biblical legal codes /15/, in inscriptional curses /16/ and in the Hittite treaties /17/.

Nevertheless, as a result of Alt's work, it became increasingly apparent that Wellhausen's dictum that the law came after the prophets was only valid in so far as the literary collection of the law was concerned. Wellhausen had failed to recognise that each collection in fact contained traditions which were much older than their present literary composition. The recognition that the basis of law went back to the very earliest stage of Israel's existence necessitated a reappraisal of the place of the prophets in Israel's development, for it became clear that they could no longer be regarded as great innovators or as the pioneers of ethical monotheism. Indeed, it came to be recognised that the prophets were not inculcating a new morality or promulgating norms which Israel did not know; on the contrary, the law provided the indispensable context for the strictures of the prophets against the people and it formed the essential presupposition of their ethical pronouncements /18/.

Another factor which necessitated a reappraisal of the significance of the prophetic teaching was the growing tendency to posit an early date for the concept of "covenant" in

Israel. The paucity of references to such a covenant in the eighth-century prophets had led earlier scholars to discount its influence on their teaching. Indeed, Wellhausen had argued that the Israelite covenant was a late invention in Israel's history which could certainly not be dated earlier than the seventh century B.C. /19/. However, the late provenance of the covenant concept was challenged by Mendenhall's discovery that certain vassal-treaties from the ancient Near East provided important material for the study of the concept of "covenant" in Israel /20/. Mendenhall was primarily concerned to demonstrate the similarity between the form and vocabulary of the Hittite vassal-treaties of the Late Bronze Age (1450-1200 B.C.) and certain passages in the Old Testament which described a covenant between Yahweh and Israel (Ex. 19-24; Josh. 24). In the ancient Near Eastern treaty, the vassal state was placed under the protection of the overlord, and the vassal, in turn, was required to accept a list of stipulations which in effect constituted the essence of the treaty. Mendenhall argued that Moses had bound Israel to Yahweh in a similar manner, and he suggested that Israel's covenant was no more than an adaptation of the form of the ancient Near Eastern suzerainty treaty. The Decalogue of Ex. 20 was regarded as the original text of the covenant between Yahweh and Israel, although Mendenhall himself recognised that the parallel with the treaty-form could not be regarded as exact, since the Decalogue lacked the list of witnesses, the blessing and curse formula and the provision for the depositing of the covenant document in the sanctuary. Nevertheless, he argued that the absence of these features in the Decalogue did not substantially weaken his theory, since these elements were to be found elsewhere in the Mosaic traditions /21/. Since the Hittite treaties represented a highly developed form known throughout the ancient Near East and since such treaties existed in pre-Mosaic times, it was suggested that they could easily have been known to Moses and used by him as a vehicle to express the relation between Yahweh and his people /22/.

As a result of Mendenhall's work, many scholars were prepared to accept the antiquity of the traditions concerning the establishing of the covenant at Sinai /23/. Indeed, some of these scholars had already argued for a Mosaic dating for Israel's covenant, and they regarded the parallels with the Hittite treaties dating from the second millennium B.C. as confirming their view /24/. Thus the possibility was open that

18

the prophets in their teaching presupposed the existence of the covenant relation between Yahweh and Israel, and used this as the basis of their proclamation of judgement /25/. The unique contribution of the prophets was not that they had formulated a new morality but that they had reawakened in the people a sense of obligation to keep the covenant relationship intact, and that they had done so in a period when it had largely been neglected and become open to abuse /26/. The prophets therefore used the concept of "covenant" to depict the relation between Yahweh and Israel, and they believed that the response of the people should be expressed in terms of obedience to the covenant laws. Some scholars went so far as to argue that not only was the treaty-form adopted in Israel to describe its special relation with Yahweh, but that the prophets themselves used basic motifs and expressions which recurred in contemporary political treaties in order to emphasise the fact that the religious and social abuses against which they inveighed were, in fact, a breach of the covenant relationship /27/. Thus, even in passages in the prophetic literature where the word berît did not occur, the idea of a covenant relationship between Yahweh and Israel may nevertheless have been implicit, since these passages were believed to reflect the type of vocabulary used in the treaties. The covenant concept, therefore, was regarded as one of the most basic influences which shaped the thought of the eighth-century prophets, and it was argued that their teaching was simply a proclamation of the ethical implications of the covenant established at Sinai.

This emphasis on the relation of the prophets to the traditions of law and covenant was undoubtedly a reaction against the views of Wellhausen and Duhm that the prophets introduced a new morality and developed a spiritual religion which owed little or nothing to tradition. The prophets were no longer regarded as being engaged in the formation of a new religion; rather, they were concerned with the radical revival of the ancient election tradition and its application to the contemporary situation. The emphasis on the new and creative element in the teaching of the prophets was giving way to attempts to ascertain the traditions which were regarded as having exercised a decisive influence upon them /28/. One of the most significant attempts to identify these traditions was made by von Rad in the second volume of his Theologie des Alten Testaments /29/ where he argued that the prophetic message was rooted in large complexes of traditions, especially those connected with the Exodus, David and Zion. According to von Rad, the Sinai covenant tradition was the ultimate basis of appeal for Amos and Hosea; in Judah, however, this covenant tradition was extended by the addition of a belief in the election by Yahweh of the house of David and Mount Zion. Yet these traditions were never wholly independent, and much of the Sinai covenant tradition continued to be a strong influence in Judah. Thus he argued that it must not be concluded from the fact that Isaiah and Micah make little reference to the complex of Exodus-Sinai events that they were ignorant of them or regarded them as of little importance, since these events were in fact presupposed in the tradition of the Davidic covenant. The four eighth-century prophets, therefore, were rooted in the sacral traditions of the early Israelite tribal federation. Von Rad recognised that the precise nature of the relation of these prophets to tradition was ambiguous, for on the one hand they were firmly implanted on the solid foundation of the ancient religious traditions and presupposed the events of the salvation history, while on the other hand they stood outside the Heils-geschichte and broke with the particular understanding of the tradition which was prevalent in Israel /30/.

Some scholars, however, regarded this emphasis on the role of tradition in the preaching of the prophets as an over-reaction against the views of Wellhausen and his contemporaries, and it was argued that to interpret the prophets simply in the light of the covenant obscured the originality of their words and reduced them merely to the level of spokesmen for, or interpreters of, the old sacral traditions. The whole issue was, of course, complicated by the fact that there was still much scholarly debate as to how early the word $b^e r\hat{\imath} t$ may be said to have been in use as a term to describe Israel's relation with Yahweh. Perlitt, for example, had argued in favour of a Deuteronomic origin for the concept of $b^e r\hat{\imath} t$ in the Old Testament /31/. Consequently, he suggested that all attempts to prove the existence of a uniform covenant ideology as a basis for the message of the prophets were futile /32/. The references to the covenant in Hos. 6:7; 8:1 were regarded as of doubtful authenticity, and it was argued that only by assuming that the covenant was a relatively late concept in Israel's religious history could one adequately explain the lack of references to it in the oracles of the eighth-century prophets /33/. The arguments of Mendenhall and others who favoured an early date for the Mosaic covenant on the basis of parallels in form and language with the vassal-treaties dating from the second millennium were dismissed on the grounds that some of the most basic elements of the treaty were lacking in the biblical material. In this regard, due weight was given to the detailed criticisms levelled by D.J. McCarthy against the facile conversion of the Hittite political treaties into the prototype of Israel's covenant with Yahweh /34/. McCarthy observed that the narrative contained in Ex. 19-24 could not be regarded as exhibiting the treaty-form, and he pointed out that some of the features which were characteristic of the treaties - such as the blessing and curse formula - were here lacking /35/. On the other hand, McCarthy did find evidence for the use of the treaty-form in the central discourse of Deuteronomy (Deut. 5-28) /36/, and this he regarded as significant, for it brought into focus the importance of the concept of "covenant" in the seventh century B.C., and the part played by the Deuteronomic movement in creating and developing a covenant theology in Israel. Indeed, all references to covenant and law in the teaching of the eighth-century prophets could be regarded as redactional, for it was the Deuteronomist who was ultimately responsible for viewing these prophets as the preachers of <u>torah</u> and as spokesmen of the covenant inaugurated by Moses on Sinai /37/.

Such a view of the relation of the prophets to tradition did not, of course, entail a return to the position advocated by Wellhausen, for it was now recognised that certain traditions were indeed available to these prophets and that only by utilising such traditions could they have made themselves intelligible to their hearers. It was essential that the prophets take a starting point familiar to their audience however much they may subsequently have departed from or reinterpreted the traditions which they used. But it was misleading to argue, as von Rad had done, that the prophets thought <u>exclusively</u> within the framework of the older traditions and that they simply adapted them to the situations which prevailed in their own day. Such an interpretation did less than justice to the charismatic nature of prophecy and to the prophet's own claim to be preaching the living word of God, as he had received it in moments of divine inspiration. Fohrer, in particular, had argued that although the prophets used older traditions, they were not entirely dependent upon them but used them to make the living word of God comprehensible to the people /38/. The decisive factor was, on the one hand, "the individual experience of the terrifying and merciful presence of God in those moments of secret experiences ... in which the spirit or the word of God came upon them", and on the other, "the living impress of the belief of the Mosaic age, which lived anew in them in a more refined and expanded form," /39/. Their God was much more the living, present God who confronted men with crucial choices than he was the God of the national religious tradition, however venerable. Thus von Rad's view that the prophets simply revitalised the traditions of the Exodus and Zion was considered dubious by Fohrer, for he felt that to regard the relation between Yahweh and Israel solely in terms of a contractual relation such as that exemplified in the concept of the covenant was to obscure the importance of the personal communion of the prophets with their God. The crucial factor for any understanding of their message, therefore, was not their connection with tradition but their own unique experience of the presence of Yahweh.

Fohrer's position was further developed by his pupil, Jochen Vollmer, who examined in some detail the historical traditions employed by Amos, Hosea and Isaiah /40/. The title of his monograph might suggest a study carried out along lines such as those suggested by von Rad and intended to reinforce the importance of tradition in the preaching of the prophets. However, Vollmer was not so much concerned to examine the presence of historical traditions in the prophets as he was to examine the purpose and motifs behind the use of such traditions. Indeed, in contradistinction to von Rad, Vollmer saw the numerous allusions to historical events in the prophets not as indicative of the fact that they were rooted in tradition but rather as indicating that they were able to use these traditions freely in order to emphasise the immanence of judgement and the end of history. Some scholars had argued that the acquaintance of the prophets with Israel's traditions - especially those of the Exodus and Settlement - provided prima facie evidence of their familiarity with, and acceptance of, the tradition of the covenant /41/. However, Vollmer demonstrated that the reference to historical traditions may have been no more than a device employed by the prophets in order to gain the general agreement of their audience. The mere fact that the prophets referred to certain traditions did not mean that they themselves necessarily accepted the validity of those traditions, for they may simply have taken the idea over from their hearers for the sake of argument. With regard to the actual events of the past, the prophet and his audience would have been in general agreement; it was in the <u>interpretation</u> of these events that they differed, for the prophet might draw radically different conclusions from premises that they held in common. Thus in Am. 3:1-2 the prophet had taken over the statement of election from his audience, and the unexpected consequence which Amos derived from it - that Yahweh would punish Israel - was intended to shock his hearers by contrast with the popular expectation that God would bless the nation. It did not follow, therefore, that Amos himself accepted the fact of Israel's election and this, indeed, would seem to be confirmed by Am. 9:7 where the prophet seems to deny that Israel held any privileged position before God /42/. Occasionally, the recollection of historical events was simply a device designed to highlight the culpability of the nation by emphasising its repeated disloyalty to Yahweh in the past (cf. Am. 4:6-11; Is. 9:8-20). The measures which God had taken to effect a restoration of Israel had been ignored and, in so far as the prophets were concerned, this served as a confirmation of the fact that the only option available to Yahweh was to destroy the nation for her recalcitrance.

Thus on the basis of his examination of the use of historical traditions in the prophets, Vollmer concluded that they were not simply traditionalists but men who conceived their duty as being to proclaim the living word of God /43/.

The problem concerning the creative contribution of the prophets has recently been broached in a somewhat different way by R.F. Melugin who has argued that form-critics have generally over-emphasised the conventional patterns of speech in the prophetic literature at the expense of those elements which could be regarded as unique and original /44/. With reference to three of Isaiah's oracles (Is. 28:7-13, 14-22; 30:15-17) he attempted to show that the prophet could sometimes employ a conventional <u>genre</u> and yet incorporate into it some features which were quite unusual. The prophet, therefore, did not always feel tied down to the typical and conventional patterns of speech; on the contrary, he used his artistic freedom to modify certain <u>genres</u>, and in doing so he placed the stamp of his own creativity on a typical form.

The above discussion would seem to indicate that the debate concerning the relation of the prophets to tradition has reached something of an <u>impasse</u>. We have seen that the views of Wellhausen and Duhm that the prophets inculcated a new

23

morality and were pioneers of ethical monotheism have since been regarded as inadequate, and their somewhat simplistic approach to the problems concerning the basis of the ethical teaching of the prophets has largely been abandoned. This in turn had given way to an interpretation of the prophets which regarded them as being bound to various complexes of tradition, although some scholars were of the view that this approach should not be over-emphasised, since it tended to obscure the originality of the prophet's own words. It now remains to examine in more detail three traditions which have been regarded as having influenced the thought of Isaiah, namely the traditions of wisdom and the law and the proposed dependence of the prophet on the oracles of his contemporary, Amos.

PART II: Traditional Elements in Isaiah

A. The Law

We have already adverted to the fact that form-critical and traditio-historical investigations into the nature and origins of Israel's legal codes suggested the early dating of the Decalogue in Israel and that this, in turn, opened up the possibility that the prophets grounded their accusations in the ancient traditions of law and covenant. However, it will be our aim in the present study to show that Isaiah's concern with social justice does not necessitate such a presupposition, and that simply to posit a legal basis for his indictments raises problems which are more difficult and complex than has generally been recognised.

It will be convenient to begin by noting the observations of von Rad concerning the relation of the prophets to the law of ancient Israel. Von Rad observes that the precepts safeguarding life, marriage and property such as those found in the Decalogue of Ex. 20 cannot be regarded as providing a complete system of rules governing all aspects of human behaviour. On the contrary, the stipulations of the Decalogue contained only the absolute minimum of Yahweh's requirements of his people, and since his demands only involved some measure of forbearance on their part, they must have been regarded as precepts which could easily have been fulfilled. Indeed, according to von Rad, it would have been quite obvious to everyone that society could not have functioned effectively unless these minimum standards of conduct were observed by the individual members of the community, and it was precisely because such commandments were so obvious that they did not require any substantiation to legitimate them before men. However, within the sphere of life circumscribed by these commandments, there lay a wide area of moral action which remained completely unregulated /1/.

According to von Rad, this understanding of the nature of the commandments is necessary if the radical preaching of the law in the eighth-century prophets is to be adequately appreciated. These prophets recognised that the rules contained in the Decalogue were necessary conditions of social and individual well-being, but they also realised that these stipulations were quite inadequate to define with any precision the moral behaviour demanded by Yahweh. Indeed, it was possible to violate certain moral principles without necessarily transgressing the law. Occasionally, of course, the demands of the Decalogue were neglected by certain individuals in the community, and in such cases the prophets based their indictments firmly on the specific legal stipulations which were being infringed. But in general, the law was regarded as easy to observe, and consequently the prophets rarely found it necessary to speak of the breach of particular commandments. Instead, they were more concerned with Israel's total failure in her relation with Yahweh. It was for this reason that the prophets were able to tear away the veil from every sphere of Israel's life and view all her actions in the light of God's demands. Thus it was not that Israel had failed to observe the commandments imposed upon her by Yahweh that concerned the prophets as much as Israel's general failure to respond to God's acts of salvation in history. In so far as the law was a gift of Yahweh's grace, contempt of that law was simply a further manifestation of Israel's general unresponsiveness towards the benefits which Yahweh had conferred upon her. For the prophets, therefore, the sins of the people arose not out of their failure to observe the individual stipulations of the law but rather out of their failure to respond to Yahweh's work of salvation.

Von Rad's observations are important, for they bring into focus the fact that obedience to the law would not in itself have been an effective means of eradicating the social abuses which were prevalent in Israel and Judah during the eighth century B.C. Certain modes of behaviour may not have been violations of the law although they may have constituted a form of conduct unbefitting a member of the covenant community. In fact, many of the practices against which the prophets inveighed came within that area of moral action which was not regulated by the law. The prophets, therefore, conceived their task as being to engender in the people an openness and generosity which would far outrun legal obligation /2/. The commandments, being predominantly negative in character, had only a limited effect in inducing men to live up to the excellence of which they were capable. Consequently, the demands of the prophets went far beyond the negative formulations of the law and they were often affirmative in nature (cf. Am. 5:6, 14f.) /3/. In this way, the prophets emphasised that although the stipulations of the law were binding and that any infringement of them would be duly punished, it was the voluntary participation of the people in acts which they themselves believed to be good, right and necessary that ultimately made it possible for the social order to function equitably.

It will be our concern in this study to develop some of von Rad's observations concerning the inadequacy of the law in combating the various social abuses which were prevalent in Israel and Judah. Indeed, it will be our contention that not only the Decalogue but the law as a whole was such a limited and imperfect instrument that serious doubts may be entertained concerning the dependence of the prophets on Israel's legal tradition.

It may be noted at the outset that many of the accusations levelled by Isaiah against his contemporaries concern certain modes of behaviour or attitudes of mind over which the law could exercise no jurisdiction. Thus, for example, as far as it is known Israel had no sumptuary laws, and if this was so, the prophet's condemnation of the people's extravagance and luxury cannot have been rooted in Israel's legal tradition. Similarly, the law did not concern itself with sobriety, and consequently the accusations against drunkenness (Is. 5:11, 22) could have had no basis in any specific legal stipulation /4/. Further, it is unlikely that Isaiah's condemnation of pride, self-gratification and vanity (Is. 3:18ff.; 5:21) were rooted in the law, for it is difficult to see how such attitudes of mind could have been effectively controlled through legislation. In such cases, conduct must be governed by mutual trust and respect rather than by strict compliance with defined obligations.

Moreover, the growth and expansion of a flourishing trade during the period of the monarchy necessitated the issuing of new stipulations if the law was to remain responsive to the changing situation. No law could be so self-sufficient or complete that it did not require to be modified occasionally to accommodate new situations. Indeed, the Old Testament itself recognises that certain cases led to the filling of gaps in the law, and the narratives concerning the daughters of Zelophehad (Num. 27:1 ff.; 35:1 ff.) /5/ and the man who collected wood on the Sabbath (Num. 15:32ff.) /6/ are particularly instructive in this regard, for both concern cases which could not be settled on the basis of existing legislation. But the enactment of new decrees may have opened up the way for economic and legal exploitation, and it may have provided a legal basis for some of the less attractive manoeuvres executed by the wealthier citizens in order to achieve their goal (cf. Is. 10:1ff.).

Further, it must be observed that there were various ways in which the law could be circumvented by these wealthier citizens in order to obtain power over the weaker members of the community. It will, in fact, be argued that some of the methods used by the rich to acquire property at the expense of the small-holders were not technically illegal, for land could have been legitimately appropriated through the foreclosure of mortgage, and its occupants may have been legally enslaved through debt-bondage /7/. The prophets were therefore often concerned with people whose conduct had never gone beyond the bounds of legality, but who were nevertheless prepared to exploit the weaknesses of the law with an unrestrained zeal. By using various legal and procedural loopholes, they were able to deprive the poor of their patrimony and force them and their families into servitude. It is clear that an appeal to the law in such cases would have added little weight to the condemnations of the prophets for, in general, they were not dealing with criminals, but simply with those who were prepared to exploit the law to their own advantage. Thus the appeals of the prophets on behalf of the indigent members of society were not all appeals for justice against men who were oppressing them illegally; some were probably appeals to those who were legally in a position to oppress them to have mercy and compassion on their pitiful state. This suggests that the prophets were often concerned not so much with actions that were illegal but simply with actions that tended to corrupt the ethos of society, whether in the form of cruelty, inhumanity or merely a failure to recognise where one's duty lay in relation to one's fellow-men. Such offences could not always be defined in precisely-formulated legal terms; instead, they had to be left to the jurisdiction of public opinion and individual conscience.

How effective, then, was the law in mitigating social abuses?

Were the provisions sufficient to ensure that those victimised by the inequalities and brutalities inherent in the social system could be protected and given fair play? To be sure, there were many laws which sought to protect the rights of the poorer members of the community; but on the other hand, it must be stated that there is often ground for scepticism regarding the effectiveness of such provisions in achieving their objectives. It may be appropriate here to instance the provision regarding the equality of all citizens before the law (Ex. 23:3, 6). According to this stipulation, every citizen was equally entitled to the protection of the law and every citizen was equally liable to conform to its requirements. Yet, it is possible to conceive of a number of ways in which this law may have failed in its purpose. In the first place, the law depended for its effectiveness on the existence of men of honesty and integrity who were able and willing to see that it was properly enforced. If the judiciary was corrupt, then the purpose of the law would have been undermined and the poor may not have been given an equitable decision. Moreover, the need for consistency in the application of the law so that similar cases were treated in a similar way may easily have resulted in injustice if no account was taken of the economic circumstances and social position of the individual litigants. Thus the law may have failed in its function simply because it had been applied too rigorously by those in a position of responsibility, and in this way the principle of "equality before the law" may have resulted in an unjust verdict even though the procedure of its administration was beyond reproach. Further, the freedom of the citizen to invoke the machinery of the law when he felt that others had impeded him without justification may have been considerably restricted by the property-owning qualification which was necessary before he could take his case to litigation /8/. Thus it must be concluded that even the laws designed to ensure the protection of the poor were not always an effective means of preventing oppression and exploitation.

Another factor which may be raised here is the extent to which the punishment prescribed for certain offences would have been an effective measure to discountenance the offence in question. If the severity of the punishment did not accord with the moral gravity of the crime, then citizens may not always have been coerced into obedience by the threat of penal sanctions /9/. In any case, as we have already observed, the wealthy could often achieve their objectives without necessarily transgressing any specific legal stipulation, and the question of punishment would therefore not have arisen.

A number of reasons have been noted above for supposing that many of the accusations levelled by Isaiah against his contemporaries were not based on specific legal provisions which can readily be identified. In the first place, it was noted that although the smooth functioning of society and the preservation of order naturally required that many activities be regulated by law, it was inevitable that not all social control could have been achieved through the legal order, since it was intrinsically impossible to legislate against certain types of conduct. Thus the condemnation of pride, extravagance and luxury could not have been rooted in Israel's legal tradition. However many and complex may have been the rules of existing law, they could not be expected to cover every possible contingency, and hence it is not surprising that the legal codes should exhibit many gaps and imperfections. This means that the law could easily have been exploited in various ways, and it was no doubt possible to pursue the most iniquitous ends and yet preserve a genuine respect for the basic principles of legality. Such considerations as these must be taken into account if the relation of the prophet to the law is to be effectively discerned. Other areas in which the law was felt to be inadequate will be developed in the course of this study, and it is precisely this fundamental inadequacy in Israel's legislation that will lead us to suggest that Isaiah's concern with social justice did not primarily involve such duties as those laid down in any particular legal code.

B. The Wisdom Tradition

Another tradition which is said to lie behind Isaiah's oracles is that of wisdom, and the purpose of this section is to discuss some of the more important contributions to the debate concerning the relation of the prophet to the circle of the wise. That some connection exists between wisdom and prophecy is a fact which has long been recognised by students of the Old Testament. The view of earlier scholars concerning the nature of this relationship was largely conditioned by their belief that wisdom only emerged in Israel at a comparatively late date. Consequently, the wise men were regarded as heirs of the prophetic tradition, and their task was to apply the profound moral insights of the prophets to the more mundane and everyday experiences of life /10/. However, the notion of the

29

late emergence of wisdom in Israel was challenged first by the application of form-criticism to the wisdom-sayings and secondly by the discovery of similar wisdom-forms among other peoples of the ancient Near East /11/. This resulted in the recognition that much of the content of the wisdom literature of the Old Testament may be early even though its final literary compilation was late /12/. Further, there was an increasing tendency to regard the traditions connecting Solomon with wisdom (1 Kings 5:21ff.; 10:1ff., 23ff.) as being historically reliable and this, too, confirmed the early provenance of wisdom in Israel /13/. Indeed, some scholars even suggested that Solomon was responsible for the existence of an influential wisdom-school in Jerusalem where young members of the court could receive their education before taking office in the administration of the state /14/. Thus there was an increasing recognition that from the early days of Solomon the literary activity of the wise men had begun to exert an influence on Israelite literature. This obviously necessitated a reappraisal of the nature of the relation between wisdom and prophecy, for the possibility was now open that it was in fact the prophets who had been influenced by traditions emanating from the circle of the wise.

Fichtner's study of the prophet Isaiah was a significant contribution to this debate, for he noted on the one hand the presence of many wisdom forms and motifs in Isaiah's oracles and on the other he detected a sharp antipathy between the prophet and the royal counsellors /15/. Fichtner sought to resolve this apparent contradiction by suggesting that Isaiah had been brought up in the court circle of Jerusalem where he had been trained as a counsellor or scribe but that later he became a prophet and rejected human counsel in favour of divine wisdom /16/. This transition was believed to have been depicted in the account of his inaugural vision as recorded in Is. 6:1 ff. As a wise man, Isaiah's task would have been to call upon men to hear, learn and understand, but his commission as a prophet was completely different, for he was now instructed to make "the heart of this people fat, and their ears heavy, and shut their eyes" (Is. 6:10) so that the people would no longer comprehend his teaching. Fichtner interpreted this to mean that Yahweh was sending the prophet on a mission the goal of which was completely contrary to that in which he had hitherto been engaged /17/. Thus the use of wisdom-sayings in Isaiah's oracles was to be accounted for by the fact that he had earlier been trained as a counsellor and that when he later became a prophet he utilised his knowledge of wisdom language in order to oppose the very milieu to which he himself had once belonged.

Although few scholars were prepared to accept Fichtner's view of Isaiah as a converted sage, his broader assertion of wisdom influence on the prophet has been more widely accepted /18/. This view has been developed in particular by J.W. Whedbee /19/, who has subjected some of Isaiah's oracles to a form-critical analysis so that the prophet's use of wisdom material may be more effectively discerned. He noted that some of the most characteristic themes which recur in Isaiah's oracles - such as his basic concern for justice and the awareness of the ill-effects of wine - indicated strong sapiential motifs, and he argued that the prophet's use of the parable (Is. 1:2f.; 5:1-7; 28:23-9) and the proverbial saying (Is. 10:15) confirmed his dependence on the wisdom tradition.

It was, perhaps, inevitable that Fichtner's study should have provoked scholars to examine the presence of the stylistic forms reminiscent of wisdom which are found in other prophets besides Isaiah /20/. Amos in particular was thought to have been indebted to the wisdom tradition, and it was suggested that certain stylistic features in his oracles - notably the rhetorical questions with a didactic purpose (Am. 3:3-8), the woe-form (Am. 5:18; 6:1) and numerical devices (Am. 1:3-2:8) - confirmed this view /21/. Indeed, Wolff found these features to be so characteristic of Amos that he argued against those scholars who had viewed the prophet in terms of a cultic background and suggested instead that Amos had been nurtured in the wisdom of the clan /22/.

Some scholars, however, felt certain reservations concerning these attempts to trace the extent of wisdom-influence on the teaching of the prophets /23/. In the first place it was pointed out that wisdom was largely concerned with universal problems which were likely to occur in any society, and hence the use of common themes and motifs in wisdom and in the prophets was hardly sufficient to indicate a dependence of one upon the other /24/. Moreover, although it could not be denied that some of the most characteristic speech-forms of the prophets frequently recurred in the wisdom literature, it did not necessarily follow that such forms represented a distinctive, technical vocabulary of wisdom which could readily be identified. The proverb, riddle and admonition were simply literary devices which were part of any society's cultural heritage, and the use of such forms by the prophets may have indicated no more than an attempt on their part to attain rhetorical effectiveness by adopting forms of speech current among the people of their day /25/. When this fact was recognised it became virtually impossible to distinguish adequately between the "popular" wisdom which was a product of every society's oral and literary heritage, and the "technical" wisdom which was nurtured by the circle of the wise. Some scholars had sought to overcome this difficulty by compiling a list of the words which recurred most frequently in the wisdom literature and which could be regarded as useful in assessing the extent of wisdom-influence on various parts of the Old Testament /26/. However, the value of such lists was felt to be limited, for the words which they contained were in such common usage that they could not be said to represent a specific literary tradition /27/.

Whedbee himself was, to some extent, aware of these difficulties, for he was forced to concede that what was often termed "technical wisdom vocabulary" was for the most part no more than the "common property of poets and speakers from time immemorial" /28/. It was for this reason that Whedbee devoted much of his study to the antipathy between Isaiah and the wise counsellors, for he believed that it was this conflict which provided one of the most important arguments for regarding Isaiah's use of wisdom-forms as having derived from the circle of the wise as opposed to popular everyday speech /29/. Whedbee suggested that this conflict arose because Yahweh's wisdom and power were held in doubt by the ruling circles of the Jerusalem court, especially by the royal wise men, and so the defence of Yahweh's wisdom was one of the prime concerns of the prophet /30/. Isaiah, therefore, in his conflict with the wise, was consciously using the language with which they themselves would have been so familiar, and by doing so he was able to enter into the arena of their own arguments and oppose the wise on their own grounds. The royal counsellors had, in fact, advocated policies which were incompatible with the Yahwistic faith and they had neglected certain doctrines which should have formed an essential part of their teaching. Among these doctrines was the concept of Yahweh's purposive action in history which always took priority over any rival human plan or counsel (cf. Prov. 19:21). However, the counsellors, in formulating their policies, had relied entirely on their own wisdom and diplomatic cleverness and had taken no account of the supreme will and purpose of Yahweh (Is. 28:14ff.; 30:1ff.; 31:1ff.). Isaiah, therefore, conceived his task as being to emphasise the wisdom of God against which no human counsel could prevail /31/. When pitted against Yahweh's plan, any rival plan, whether that of Judah (Is. 29:15f.; 30:1ff.), Assyria (Is. 10:5ff.) or any other nation (Is. 7:3ff.; 8:9f.; 19:1ff.), was doomed to failure. Whedbee suggested that Isaiah had appropriated this concept of Yahweh's "plan" ($^{c}\bar{e}\underline{s}\bar{a}h$) from the wisdom tradition (cf. Prov. 19:21), and by doing so he attempted to convict the wise men on the basis of principles which they themselves should have embraced /32/. The prophet realised that the most effective way of accomplishing this was by using speech-forms which were proverbial in character and which, therefore, would have been familiar to his hearers. Thus, for example, Isaiah utilised the "parable of the farmer" (Is. 28:23ff.) in order to persuade the counsellors that Yahweh, too, was wise, since he also varied his activities according to the demands of the particular situation /33/. According to Whedbee, therefore, Isaiah's use of wisdom is to be viewed as part of his polemic against the wisdom-circles of his day, for he opposed the counsellors by using their own vocabulary and drawing upon their own traditions.

A somewhat different approach to the problem has been adopted by William McKane, although he, too, recognised the importance of the passages which referred to the conflict between the prophets and the wise men if any adequate assessment was to be made regarding the significance of the wisdom traditions in the prophetic literature /34/. McKane suggested that the contexts in which the word $\underline{h}^{a}k\bar{a}m\hat{i}m$ appeared made it clear that the term referred to politicians whose duty it was to advise the king on matters of diplomatic alliances and foreign policies. Thus the term did not designate the circle of the wise whose task it was to nurture wisdom and to inculcate understanding among men; rather, the $\underline{h}^{a}k\bar{a}m\hat{i}m$ were those who occupied eminent positions in the government of Judah. Such officers may have included the $\underline{s\bar{a}r\hat{i}m}$ or the $\underline{s\bar{o}p^{e}r\hat{i}m}$, and it was only in so far as these were considered to have been specially endowed with wisdom that they were referred to as the $\underline{h}^{a}k\bar{a}m\hat{i}m$ /35/. These officials were entirely secular and utilitarian in their outlook, and they were opposed by the prophets precisely because they took no account of Yahweh's sovereignty in history /36/. However, their failure in this regard was not due to the fact that they had neglected certain key concepts in their traditions; rather, it was to be accounted for by the fact that they had embraced a tradition which was itself profane and devoid of theological insight. McKane therefore argued that early wisdom had no religious content whatsoever and that it was only towards the end of the monarchy that the sages began to come to terms with the affirmations of the Yahwistic faith /37/. Thus the conflict as McKane saw it was between the divine will as revealed to the prophets on the one hand and the secular empiricism of the counsellors on the other.

Although McKane's attempt to analyse in detail the passages which reflect the conflict between the prophets and the wise men must be regarded as commendable, some of his more general conclusions must be viewed with caution. Thus, for example, his argument that old wisdom was entirely secular and eudaemonistic must remain doubtful, since von Rad has demonstrated that even the earliest wisdom presupposed a belief in the existence of an order in the world which had been created by Yahweh and which was sustained and controlled by him. Wisdom was therefore concerned with the divine realm very directly, since it was believed that every Israelite encountered the divine order in the course of his life. On the basis of this assumption, von Rad concluded that nearly all wisdom was implicitly theological and that even the experiential insights of the wise were ultimately apprehended through faith /38/. If von Rad's view concerning the theological nature of early wisdom is correct, then it is probable that the wise men were not so radically humanistic in their approach as McKane seems to suggest. Thus to argue, as he does, that the sages simply inculcated a spirit of worldly wisdom which was not profoundly religious, would be to do them a great injustice, for it is likely that their teaching was from the beginning grounded in religion.

Further, it is by no means certain that all the references to the $h^akāmîm$ can be taken to indicate an identifiable group within society. In this regard, R.N. Whybray has discussed all the passages that might conceivably suggest the use of the word $h^akāmîm$ as a designation of a professional class of wise men, and he has expressed grave doubts concerning the existence of such an institution in Israel /39/. In particular, he has emphasised that in no historical narrative in the Old Testament can the word $h^akāmîm$ be taken to refer to a group of persons connected with the court, and he regards it as

significant that in the list of royal officials found in 2 Sam.
8:16-18; 20:23-6; 1 Kings 4:2-6 there is no mention of the
ḥᵃkāmîm as a class of officials in the service of the king
/40/. Indeed Whybray concludes that it is merely the relative
frequency with which the word occurs in political contexts in
Isaiah that has misled scholars into considering that it has a
technical meaning /41/.

Whybray's conclusions, if correct, would obviously have an
important bearing on the studies of both Whedbee and McKane,
for it would mean that Isaiah was not engaged in a controversy
with a specific class known as the "wise" but that he was rather
merely concerned with the ordinary citizens in the community
who claimed to possess superior wisdom and insight. However,
Whybray goes too far in seeking to divest every trace of a
"professional" nuance from the term ḥᵃkāmîm, for certain
passages would seem to suggest that the wise did appear
together as an identifiable group in society along with the
prophets and the priests (cf. Jer. 18:18) /42/. Thus it is
reasonable to infer that when the term ḥākām or ḥᵃkāmîm
occurs in a "political" context (cf. Is. 29:14; 31:2) the word does
in fact refer to the class of royal counsellors or political
advisors employed in the court of the king. In this regard,
McKane's view that the political advisors were called
ḥᵃkāmîm by virtue of their political sagacity and their
expertise in matters of diplomacy may be sustained. However,
his argument that the conflict between Isaiah and the wise men
simply reflected a clash between the religious outlook of the
prophet and the secular, anthropocentric views of the wise must
be rejected, for it is more probable that it was the actual
policies which were being advocated by the politicians that
drew forth Isaiah's accusations /43/.

It has been necessary to discuss the conflict between Isaiah
and the wise at some length because it was this conflict,
according to Whedbee, which provided the main motivation for
Isaiah's use of the technical wisdom vocabulary with which the
circle of the wise would have been so familiar. Isaiah had
appropriated wisdom traditions in order to do battle with the
sages on their own ground, and by using the very vocabulary and
ideas of the wise he was able to remind them that Yahweh's
plan would prevail despite all the rival policies advocated by
the counsellors. But although we may agree that the prophet
was opposing an identifiable group within society which could
be designated as the "wise", it must be emphasised that this

still falls short of demonstrating the prophet's use of a "technical wisdom vocabulary". As has already been indicated, there is much wisdom hidden in the interstices of everyday speech, and such forms as the parable or proverb could be used by any speaker for the sake of rhetorical effectiveness, irrespective of whether or not he belonged to the select circle of the "wise". It must be concluded, therefore, that no clear line of demarcation can be drawn between "popular" wisdom which was an intrinsic part of Israel's cultural heritage and the more "technical" wisdom which can be traced to a distinct Sitz im Leben in the teaching of the wise men. Once this fact is recognised, the whole setting of wisdom becomes much broader, and questions concerning the possibility of wisdom-influence on a prophet become more difficult to resolve.

C. Dependence on Amos

In addition to Isaiah's dependence on the legal and wisdom traditions, it has been argued that he was also indebted to the prophetic tradition itself, since many points of similarity have been noted between the oracles of Isaiah and those of his contemporary, Amos. The implications of this have been fully expounded by Reinhard Fey who argued that the similarity between the two prophets could be satisfactorily explained only on the assumption that the oracles of Amos were familiar to Isaiah and that the latter had developed certain themes found in the teaching of his contemporary /44/. Since this theory has been accepted by a number of scholars /45/, it will be necessary to look more closely at some of the arguments which have been advanced in favour of such a view.

In the first place, it must be admitted that there is no a priori reason why Isaiah could not have known of the teaching of his contemporary, since it is probable that the oracles of the prophets were committed to writing shortly after they had been proclaimed orally /46/. However, it will be suggested in the course of the present study that Fey's thesis concerning the influence of Amos on Isaiah cannot be sustained for a variety of reasons. Our purpose in this section will simply be to discuss briefly some of the arguments which Fey has advanced in support of his view that Isaiah's condemnation of drunkenness in Is. 5:11-13 is dependent upon the similar indictment found in Am. 6:1-7. These passages have been selected for discussion here because they are the ones used by Fey himself in the opening chapter of his book as a test case to prove the validity

36

of his overall thesis /47/.

It may be noted at the outset that Fey's argument is based on the similarity in form and content between Am. 6:1-7 and Is. 5:11-13. With regard to the <u>form</u> of the two passages, he observes that both contain a long rebuke and a concise threat, that both are introduced by the particle lākēn, and that both rebukes are introduced by the word hôy. Moreover, both passages contain a long preface which is formulated in positive terms (Am. 6:1-6a; Is. 5:11-12a) and both contain a shorter, negative <u>Nachsatz</u> (Am. 6:6b; Is. 5:12b). Further, both passages exhibit a stylistic similarity in their alternation between participle and finite verbal forms. Turning to the similarity in <u>content</u> between the two passages, Fey observes that the account of the situation given by both prophets is very vivid; Amos mentions specific occurrences in the scene of the activity (they lie down, eat, drink and play instruments), and Isaiah similarly singles out certain characteristics of their revelry such as the drinking of wine and the satisfaction induced through hearing the sound of musical instruments. Fey suggests that Isaiah often expands some statements taken from his prototype and he notes an example of this in the passages under discussion. In Am. 6:5 there is simply the vague reference to the kᵉlê-šîr, but Isaiah develops this further by noting the particular instruments which were used, and only his reference to the <u>nebel</u> was actually taken from his <u>Vorlage</u>. Fey further notes that Amos' rebuke is infected with a flavour of irony, for the complacent ones who are the "notable men of the first of the nations" (Am. 6:1b) will be punished by being the "first" to go into exile (Am. 6:7a). A similar irony is encountered in Is. 5:11-13, for those who drink and feast in merriment will be the very ones who will die of hunger and be parched with thirst (Is. 5:13). Fey regards it as especially significant that the punishment mentioned in both passages is exile, and he emphasises that the same word (gālāh) is used by both prophets.

Thus Fey concludes that the parallels between Am. 6:1-7 and Is. 5:11-13 indicate beyond any doubt that Isaiah was familiar with and influenced by the teaching of Amos. He maintains that the similar vistas of thought and the similarity in construction and content can hardly be fortuitous and that they can only be adequately explained by assuming that Isaiah utilised an Amos <u>Vorlage</u>.

However, Fey's arguments are not as compelling as they may at first appear. That some similarity should exist between Am.

6:1-7 and Is. 5:11-13 is hardly surprising, for both prophets are here using the same literary form, namely the woe-oracle /48/. Since this particular Gattung almost invariably includes an interjection, a participle or substantive, an indictment and a decree of punishment, it is only to be expected that these elements should recur in the two passages under discussion. It may also be noted that the particle lākēn often follows the woe and is used to introduce the punishment which is about to overtake the people (cf. Is. 5:24; Mic. 2:3). Nor is the similarity in content as impressive as Fey suggests. He himself concedes that neither the word ᶜammî nor the phrase mibbᵉlî-dāᶜat in Is. 5:11-13 have any direct parallel in Am. 6:1-7. Further, a threat of exile (gālāh) is comparatively common in prophetic oracles (cf. Am. 5:5, 27; 7:11, 17), and consequently too much significance should not be attached to the fact that an exile is threatened in the two passages in question.

Finally, some considerations of a more general nature may be made concerning the validity of Fey's overall thesis. The weakness of Fey's approach emerges from his failure to give due recognition to the fact that both Amos and Isaiah were participating in much the same cultural and religious situation. The sins mentioned by the prophets - oppression, cruelty, exploitation, greed, dishonesty - would no doubt have been as prevalent in Judah as they were in Israel. Moreover, the social circumstances and national conditions were not essentially different in the two states, and it is hardly surprising, therefore, that the offences which were perpetrated in Israel and Judah were not only of a similar nature but also evoked a similar response from both prophets. Amos and Isaiah belonged to a society where the rich led lives of luxury and revelry, where many were arrogant and over-confident, and where there was little concern for the plight of the poor and under-privileged. These factors alone are sufficient to account for the similarities between the two prophets and it must be concluded, therefore, that the points of contact between Amos and Isaiah noted by Fey fall short of demonstrating a clear dependence of one prophet upon the other.

Conclusion

In this chapter we have been concerned to trace the main lines of interpretation which have affected the study of the Old Testament prophets since the days of Wellhausen and Duhm, and particular attention has been paid to the way in which scholars have viewed the relation of the prophets to the ancient traditions of Israel. It was indicated that scholars are by no means unanimous in their views regarding the extent to which these traditions could be said to have influenced the prophetic material. It therefore seemed appropriate to examine again the traditional elements which have been thought to underlie the prophetic material, and the oracles of Isaiah provided a convenient basis for our discussion, since he is said to have been influenced by the legal and wisdom traditions of Israel, as well as by the prophetic tradition itself. It has been our aim in this chapter simply to highlight some of the difficulties which inevitably arise when Isaiah is viewed against such a traditionary background. In the following chapters we shall endeavour to examine in more detail the influence of tradition on the prophet by analysing some of the passages in Isaiah where social and ethical problems predominate. In this way, it is hoped that some conclusion may be reached regarding the basis of Isaiah's ethical teaching.

Chapter Two

ISRAEL'S REBELLION AGAINST YAHWEH (Is. 1:2-3)

2   Hear, O heavens, and give ear, O earth;
        for the Lord has spoken:
    "I have reared[a] and brought up[b] sons,
        but they have rebelled against me.
3   The ox knows its owner,
        and the ass its master's[c] stall;
    Israel[d] does not know,[e]
        my people[d] does not understand".

a.   The verb גדל in the Pi‍cel (lit. "to make great") often has the meaning of "rearing children" (cf. Is. 23:4; 49:21; 51:18; 2 Kings 10:6; Hos. 9:12), and it is in this sense that the verb should be understood in the present context. Some commentators prefer here the rendering of the LXX ἐγεννησα ("have begotten") which perhaps presupposes a form of the root ילד (Scott, Kissane). However, it is not necessary to emend the text, and the reading of MT should be retained.

b.   The verb רום in the Po‍clel usually means "to promote" or "to exalt", and this is the sense attributed to the word in the present context by the LXX (ὕψωσα) and the Vulgate (exaltavi), where the reference is presumably to the greatness of Israel among the nations. However, it seems more probable that the verb should here assume the sense which it has in Is. 23:4 "bring up, rear", where it also occurs in parallel with the root גדל (cf. BDB, p.927).

c.   The plural suffix in the word בעליו is a "plural of majesty", and is quite regular (G-K §124 i).

d.   Some of the Versions suggest that a conjunction should be added before the word ישראל, and another conjunction before עמי (LXX, Syr. and Vulg.). But although this would have the advantage of setting the contrast between Israel's behaviour and that of the animals in a sharper focus, it is not necessary to emend MT.

e.   The verb ידע lacks an object, and R. Lowth, on the basis of the renderings of the LXX (Ἰσραηλ δε με οὐκ ἐγνω) and the Vulgate (Israel autem me non cognovit), has suggested that an original אותי has been lost from the Hebrew text (Isaiah, London, 1778, p.5). But the parallel use of התבונן in the absolute supports MT, and the lack of an object may simply be a device designed to broaden the scope of the accusation.

Introduction

It is probable that vv.2-26 contain a group of five originally independent oracles, and the individual units may be delineated as follows: vv.2-3, 4-9, 10-17, 18-20 and 21-6 /1/. Fohrer suggests that the compiler of these oracles arranged them partly on the basis of similarity in form and content between the individual units, and partly on the "catchword" principle which served as a convenient connecting link between the various oracles in the chapter. The five oracles, taken together, would then form a systematic composition with a progressing train of thought: vv.2-3 are concerned with the theme of "sin", and this is followed in vv.4-9 by a pronouncement of judgement; vv.10-17 hold out the possibility of deliverance; vv.18-20 present a choice between judgement and deliverance, while the possible realisation of this deliverance is expressed in vv.21-6. This sequence, according to Fohrer, is by no means accidental, but has been deliberately chosen in order to give an overall view of Isaiah's preaching. Thus the collection can be characterised as a comprehensive survey of the prophet's message as the editors have understood it /2/.

Commentators are by no means unanimous, however, in regarding vv.2-3 as a single unit, for some consider the unit to consist of vv.2-9, either because of the similarity of themes between vv.2-3 and vv.4-9 or because of the supposed cultic setting of the entire speech /3/. But a form-critical study of the chapter reveals that vv.2-9 represent two distinct Gattungen, for vv.2-3 are thought to have been patterned after the opening of a legal trial /4/, whereas the introductory hôy in v.4 would seem to mark off the following section as a reproach. Moreover, it has been pointed out that the rhythm is different in the two sections, for in vv.2-3 the metre is 3:3, whereas in the lament over the destruction of the land that follows in vv.4-9, the metre varies between 3:2 and 2:2 /5/. Further, the change from the first person speech of Yahweh in vv.2-3 to the third person speech about Yahweh in v.4 suggests that this verse opens a new section. Thus on the grounds of form, content and metre it may be assumed that vv.2-3 are a separate unit.

It will be our concern in the discussion that follows to examine the traditions which have been thought to underlie these verses. The three different traditions which have been suggested include a background in the covenant or in the vassal-treaties of the ancient Near East, a legal background and a background in the wisdom literature /6/. These three traditions will here be discussed separately, although it should be emphasised at the outset that these traditions are by no means regarded as being mutually exclusive, for some would adhere to the view that both "legal" and "wisdom" concepts underlie this passage /7/, while others would maintain that a background in wisdom and in the vassal-treaty is not incompatible /8/.

A. The Background in the Treaty and Covenant

An investigation into the covenantal and treaty background of Is. 1:2-3 must begin with Mendenhall's claim that the form lying behind the covenant established between Yahweh and Israel at Sinai was that of the suzerainty treaty between an emperor and his vassal, the best examples of which come from the Hittite empire of the Late Bronze Age /9/. The form of these treaties can, of course, vary but, allowing for the vagaries of historical transmission, certain stable features can be recognised. These features have been outlined by Mendenhall /10/ as follows:

1. The preamble, in which the king identifies himself and in which his titles and attributes are listed together with his genealogy.
2. The historical prologue, which contains a description of the previous relationships between the contracting parties.
3. The obligations binding on the vassal are listed.
4. A clause is provided for the treaty document to be deposited in the sanctuary of the vassal and to be read in public from time to time.
5. The gods who witnessed the making of the treaty are listed.
6. Blessings and curses are listed to ensure that the vassal obeys the stipulations of the treaty.

Mendenhall emphasised that the Hittites themselves did not

create this treaty-form; rather, it was to be regarded as an already well-established form in the ancient Near East, and one which derived ultimately from Mesopotamia. The form would consequently have been familiar to various states during the second millennium B.C. /11/. It was conceivable, therefore, that this form would have been known to Moses and utilised by him in order to depict the nature of the relationship established between Yahweh and Israel on Sinai /12/.

An investigation into the precise nature of the relation between the covenant established at Sinai and the ancient Near Eastern vassal-treaties would transgress the limits of this chapter, and consequently it will be necessary in the discussion that follows to confine ourselves to the view that much of Isaiah's teaching takes on a new significance when it is seen against the background of the treaty between a suzerain and his vassal. The oracle with which Isaiah's prophecy opens (Is. 1:2-3) will provide a convenient focus for our discussion, since this oracle is often interpreted in terms of ideas and expressions prevalent in the vassal-treaties.

1. Invocation of Heaven and Earth

It has already been observed that one of the recurring features of the vassal-treaty was the list of gods who were invoked as witnesses and as guarantors of the treaty /13/. That the treaty terms were ratified in the presence of divine witnesses is attested, for example, by the vassal-treaty between Esarhaddon, the king of Assyria, and a chieftain of the Medes named Ramataia. This document contains a long list of deities, and it is clear that they are present in order to be witnesses to the treaty and to the vassal's affirmation of its terms /14/. A similar list of gods occurs in an Aramaic vassal-treaty dating from the eighth century B.C. which was made between Bar-ga'ayah, king of KTK, and Mati^{c}el, king of Arpad /15/. After the list of gods, the treaties often contain references to mountains, rivers, heaven and earth, and various other cosmic phenomena. This feature appears, for example, in the treaty of Duppi-Teššub where a long list of the gods of the land of Ḫatti and the gods of the land of Amurru is followed by a reference to "the mountains, the rivers, the springs, the great Sea, heaven and earth, the winds (and) the clouds" /16/. Similarly, in an Egyptian treaty between Rameses II and Ḫattušili, a thousand male and female gods of the land of Egypt are called upon as "witnesses", and there follows a reference to "the mountains and the rivers of the land of Egypt; the sky; the earth; the great sea; the winds; the clouds" /17/.

Mendenhall observed that no exact parallel to the list of deities could be expected to occur in the Israelite tradition, for the first commandment (Ex. 20:3) precluded the possibility of an appeal to other gods as witnesses to the covenant ceremony. It was inevitable, therefore, that in the traditions connected with Sinai, Yahweh himself should appear not only as a party to the covenant but also as a guarantor of that covenant, and this clearly obviated the necessity of any appeal to a third party /18/. But although the list of witnesses was lacking in the account of the establishment of the covenant at Sinai, Mendenhall believed that this feature of the vassal-treaties had been preserved in certain passages in the Old Testament where an appeal was made to "heaven and earth" as witnesses in the controversy between Yahweh and his people (cf. Deut. 32:1; Is. 1:2) /19/.

It is on the basis of this observation by Mendenhall that some commentators have viewed the invocation of "heaven and earth" in Is. 1:2a against a background in the covenant- or treaty-form /20/. The words "Hear, O heavens and give ear, O earth" are regarded as an appeal to the witnesses who were present when Yahweh concluded the covenant with Israel. Should the threats implicit in that covenant materialise, then heaven and earth are witnesses to the fact that Israel has not been faithful to her covenant obligations, and that Yahweh is therefore not acting improperly in bringing punishment upon the people. Thus the appeal to "heaven and earth" is taken to indicate a covenantal or treaty background /21/, and consequently it is assumed that when this appeal occurs in the prophetic literature, the device was deliberately used by the prophets to evoke in their audience the notion of the covenant and to express in vivid terms the "indictment and trial of Israel because of unfulfilled covenant obligations" /22/.

However, it cannot be assumed that the mere invocation of "heaven and earth" automatically indicates a treaty or covenantal background, for a similar invocation is encountered in other contexts, too, such as in the Sumerian and Akkadian exorcism formulae /23/, and in various prayers /24/ and hymns of praise /25/. Moreover, within the Old Testament itself, heaven and earth function in a variety of different settings. Sometimes they are commanded to rejoice before Yahweh (cf. Ps. 96:11; Is. 44:23; 49:13), sometimes they are called upon to mourn (cf. Jer. 4:28), and sometimes they are invoked simply to render praise to God (cf. Ps. 69:35). This does not, of course, preclude the possibility that heaven and earth could function in specifically covenantal contexts in the Old Testament (cf. Deut. 4:26; 30:19; 31:28) /26/, but it must be emphasised that the mere reference to "heaven and earth" does not in itself constitute sufficient evidence to warrant the conclusion that the context in which it appears is to be understood against a background in the treaties of the ancient Near East.

Thus it seems rather venturesome to draw a direct line of dependence from the references to "heaven and earth" in the vassal-treaties to the use of the similar expression in Is. 1:2. As Fohrer has observed, the reference to "heaven and earth" in this passage is too far removed from the deified nature-powers which are enumerated in the international treaties for one to be able to posit a link between the two /27/. If a connection is posited, however, it would be necessary to suppose that the deification of natural phenomena in the treaties has here been cleansed of all mythological connotations in order to make it consonant with Israel's faith. But it is hardly necessary to assert such a hypothesis, and the invocation of "heaven and earth" by Isaiah may indicate nothing more than an appeal to the natural world to hear Yahweh's judgement.

2. Israel's Rebellion against Yahweh

Some scholars have approached the treaty background of Is. 1:2-3 from a different vantage point by suggesting that the words "I have reared and brought up sons, but they have rebelled against me" (v.2) reflect the thought and terminology of the international treaties. The phrase is interpreted to mean that Yahweh has bestowed blessings upon his children by delivering them from Egypt and that this act constitutes the basis of Israel's obligations towards its benefactor. This is said to correspond in some measure with the "preamble" and "historical prologue" of the Hittite treaties where great emphasis was placed on the benevolent deeds which the Hittite king had performed for the benefit of the vassal who was, in turn, obligated to perpetual gratitude towards the suzerain /28/. Thus Yahweh, the covenant God of Israel, is given a position which is similar to that of the Near Eastern suzerain, and Israel is to render him the obedience and undivided loyalty of a vassal /29/.

In this regard, the use of the word "sons" (bānîm) in Is. 1:2 is thought to be particularly significant, for there is evidence to indicate that, outside Israel, the community constituted by a treaty was characterised by terms derived from the sphere of family relationships /30/. The unity established by the treaty was thereby equated with the firmness of the blood-bond. Thus in the vassal-treaties, "sonship" (marûtum) was a concept which was often used to express subordination, especially that of a vassal to his overlord or "father" /31/. D.J. McCarthy has suggested that certain biblical passages where the "father-son" analogy appears (Deut. 32:19f.; Is. 1:2; Jer. 3:19; Mal. 1:6) are to be interpreted in the light of the technical vocabulary of the treaties, where the superior partner was called "father", his inferior "son", and equal partners, "brothers" /32/. He finds support for his theory in such passages as Is. 30:1, where the "sons" are condemned because they have turned to a stranger for help, and this is said to provide a close parallel with the central element in the treaty-relationships, namely the suzerain's claim to an exclusive fidelity from the vassal which forbade all serious dealings with outsiders /33/. The words contained in Ex. 4:22, which state that Israel was Yahweh's first-born son, are also regarded as significant in this discussion, for it has been suggested that this passage not only preserves the earliest explicit reference to the father-son relationship in the Old Testament, but that it also seems to indicate that the concept of Israel as Yahweh's "son" was closely connected with the Exodus-tradition, and thus related to the nexus of events surrounding the establishment of the covenant at Sinai /34/.

It must now be considered whether Isaiah's use of familial imagery in Is. 1:2-3 necessarily presupposes a covenantal or treaty background, and whether his emphasis on Yahweh's benevolent attitude towards Israel is to be viewed in terms of the "preamble" or "historical prologue" of the vassal-treaties of the ancient Near East.

In the first place, it must be observed that the words "I have reared and brought up sons" in Is. 1:2 need not necessarily be taken to indicate Yahweh's work in redeeming Israel from Egypt, for it is possible that the words were intended to refer only to the people of Isaiah's own day, in which case the phrase would have no "historical" reference. In this regard, it is significant that when familial imagery is used in the Old Testament to refer to those who came from Egypt, the singular bēn is used (e.g. Hos. 11:1). Here, however, Isaiah uses the plural form bānîm (cf. Is. 1:4; 30:1, 9), and it is possible that he used the plural form in order to avoid close association with pagan ideas which were well known in Israel /35/. It may be concluded, therefore, that the words bānîm giddaltî wᵉrômamtî wᵉhēm pāšᵉᶜû bî need not imply a recital of Yahweh's benevolent acts in history, and the brevity of the phrase and its vagueness /36/ suggest that it does not correspond to the lengthy "historical prologues" of the treaties.

Further, it is doubtful whether the father-son imagery need necessarily be interpreted in terms of the vocabulary derived from the vassal-treaties. It is clear that the notion of Israel's divine sonship is very ancient, and although the first explicit reference to Israel as Yahweh's son is found in Ex. 4:22, the concept is also implicit in the Song of Moses (Deut. 32:5, 6, 18, 19), a passage which probably dates from a very early period /37/. In fact, it is likely that the notion of Israel's sonship antedates the exodus from Egypt, for proper names such as Abibaal ("my father is Baal"), Abiel ("my father is El"), Joab ("Yahweh is my father") and Abijah ("my father is Yahweh") suggest that the ultimate origin of the image of God as the "father" of his people is to be traced back to the patriarchal, semi-nomadic society of the Semites in the third and second millennium /38/. In such a society, the relationship between the clan or family and its god was very close, and the family deity was considered an actual member of the clan and addressed as "father", "brother" or "kindred". Even in the earliest times, therefore, it was realised that in order to speak meaningfully about the relation between God and man, it was necessary to employ the same categories that were used to describe human relationships, and one of the most basic relationships in the experience of man was that between a father and his child.

It is clear, therefore, that the "father-son" motif is quite independent of the covenant concept. Indeed, it is possible that the "father-son" metaphor was used by Isaiah to emphasise the fact that the relation between Yahweh and Israel went far deeper than anything that could be defined in purely legal or contractual terms. It involved a relationship of the highest order with a reciprocal faithfulness of a type that was seldom found among the suzerains and vassals of the ancient Near East. While it is true that the "father-son" analogy was used in the treaties to describe the relationship between an overlord and his vassal, it would be somewhat precipitate to assume a direct link with Isaiah's use of similar imagery, for it was characteristic of the religious mind in every age to attempt to visualise God - and man's relation to him - in terms which were derived from social relationships. In this regard, it is significant that the "father-son" metaphor is only one analogy out of many used by the prophets to describe the relationship between Yahweh and Israel (cf. master-servant, husband-wife, creator-creature, redeemer-redeemed, etc.). By using such metaphors, the prophets were able to emphasise the living relationship between the people and their God, a relationship which went far beyond the formal and judicial aspects of covenant and treaty.

Some further support for the covenantal setting of the words "I have reared and brought up sons, but they have rebelled against me" in v.2 has been adduced from the use of the verb pāšaᶜ in this context. In the ancient Near Eastern treaties, the verb "rebel" was used as a term to designate a neglect to acknowledge the authority of the suzerain by violating the stipulations of the pact that bound the two parties together /39/. The term is employed in a similar way in some contexts in the Old Testament, where it is used to refer to a breach of covenant-relationships. In 1 Kings 12:16ff., for example, the murder of the king's official and the implied rejection of royal authority is termed pāšaᶜ (cf. 2 Kings 1:1; 3:5, 7; 8:20, 22). In fact, it has been thought that the term pāšaᶜ belonged primarily to the language of politics, and in such contexts designated a "revolt" or "rebellion" from one's ruler /40/. The verb has been interpreted in this way in Is. 1:2, for it is supposed that the idea underlying the passage is the rebellion of Israel against Yahweh, her covenant partner /41/.

However, this argument must be viewed with some caution, for the use of the word pāšaᶜ is too broad and general to necessitate the presupposition that it is based on the language of the treaties and international alliances. Although the root pšᶜ may suggest a rebellion against an earthly overlord, the word is often used by the prophets in a very general way of offences which have been committed against Yahweh, whether these took the form of relying upon Egypt and Assyria (cf. Hos. 7:13), or simply of being unjust and inhumane (cf. Am. 5:12). In fact, in many Old Testament texts, nothing but the most general sense of the root pšᶜ can be established (e.g. Job 14:17; Ps. 19:14), and in the absence of more decisive evidence to the contrary, it may be assumed that it is in this general sense in which the verb is to be interpreted in the present context /42/.

3. Israel's Lack of Discernment

An additional argument favouring the covenantal or treaty background of Is. 1:2-3 has been adduced from the words yiśrā'ēl lō' yādaᶜ ᶜammî lō' hitbônān in v.3b, for it has been suggested that the Hebrew verb yādaᶜ is to be regarded in some biblical texts as a technical term which corresponds to the technical usage of the Hittite sak- and Akkadian idû ("know") in the international treaties. These words, when used in such contexts, may either imply a mutual recognition on the part of the suzerain and the vassal, or they may simply denote a recognition of the treaty-stipulations as binding /43/. On the basis of this observation, it has been suggested that the verb yādaᶜ in Is. 1:3b is a covenant term which finds its closest parallel in the vassal-treaties of the ancient Near East /44/.

However, there is no reason to suppose that yādaᶜ should be interpreted in this way in the present context, for it is clear that it is the example set by the animals in v.3a that should be decisive for our understanding of the verb in v.3b /45/. The meaning would then simply be that Israel was devoid of the natural instincts with which even dumb animals were endowed /46/. Thus "to know" in this context has essentially the same meaning as the verb has in Jer. 8:7, where the prophet makes the point that migrating birds "know" (yādaᶜ) the times of their coming and leaving but that Israel did not "know" (yādaᶜ) Yahweh's ordinances. It is in this sense that the verb yādaᶜ should be understood in Is. 1:3b, and the meaning is that even the ox and ass recognise a master's care and know their way to the place where they are fed, whereas Israel does not discern any dependence upon Yahweh, since it lacks both the immediate knowledge acquired by instinct, and the discerning knowledge acquired by reflection (hitbônān). Since there is nothing of a specifically treaty or covenantal character about this, it is doubtful whether the word yādaᶜ should be interpreted in the light of its meaning in the international treaties.

4. The Covenant Lawsuit

We may conclude our investigation into the covenantal and treaty background of Is. 1:2-3 by examining the view that these verses are to be designated as a "covenant lawsuit" /47/. If this view can be sustained, it could be regarded as providing an important argument for interpreting these verses against a background in the treaty or covenant /48/. Indeed, it might even be concluded from the prophet's use of this Gattung that Isaiah was in fact impeaching Israel for a breach of covenant obligations /49/.

The essential components of the prophetic rîb have been delineated by G.E. Wright /50/ as follows:

1. A call to witnesses to listen to the proceedings.
2. A statement of the case at issue introduced by the divine judge or his earthly official.
3. A recital of the benevolent acts of the divine suzerain.
4. The indictment.
5. The sentence.

Can this form be said to underlie the oracle in Is. 1:2-3? To what extent are the elements delineated by Wright exhibited in these verses? The invocation of "heaven and earth" in Is. 1:2-3 - and in other passages which are designated as "covenant lawsuits" - is sometimes regarded as an appeal to witnesses to hear the proceedings /51/. However, it must be emphasised that there is nothing in Is. 1:2-3 to indicate that these cosmic entities are to function as "witnesses" in this particular context /52/. Further, although an accusation is brought against Israel in Is. 1:2b, there is no indication that Yahweh in this context appears in his capacity as a "judge" /53/. Moreover, it is by no means certain that the words bānîm giddaltî wᵉrômamtî wᵉhēm pāšᵉCû bî in v.2b should be taken to refer to Yahweh's benevolent acts in history, since it is possible that the people who have rebelled against Yahweh were the prophet's own contemporaries, in which case the phrase would contain no "historical" reference /54/. Finally, it may be observed that although these verses contain an indictment of Israel for her obduracy and recalcitrance, no sentence is decreed /55/.

It is clear, therefore, that some of the essential elements which constitute the "covenant lawsuit" as delineated above by Wright are lacking in Is. 1:2-3. Some scholars, aware that the essential components of the "covenant lawsuit" are missing in these verses, have maintained that the entire first chapter, or various sections therein, should be taken as exhibiting the characteristic features of this form /56/. However, in doing so, they simply ignore the clear distinctions in form and content within this chapter. It must be concluded, therefore, that it is doubtful whether Is. 1:2-3 can be designated as a "covenant lawsuit", and that it is futile to attempt to construct such a "lawsuit" by combining the disparate elements which are included within this first chapter.

B. The Legal Background

It will be our concern here to consider the view which has been advanced by various scholars that the <u>form</u> of Is. 1:2-3 was patterned after the opening of a legal trial, and that Isaiah was here utilising the forms of speech used in the legal proceedings "at the gate" in order to express Yahweh's accusation against Israel /57/. In this particular context, the prophet is said to function as a court official (<u>Gerichtsdiener</u>) who demands the attention of witnesses ("heaven and earth"), and proclaims Yahweh's judgement /58/. Thus the oracle is again designated as a "lawsuit" (<u>Gerichtsrede</u>), but this <u>Gattung</u> is thought to have derived not from the secular treaty documents, but rather from the ordinary, everyday judicial procedure in Israel /59/.

The question with which we shall be particularly concerned is whether the <u>form</u> of the indictment presented in Is. 1:2-3 corresponds to the procedure in the normal court of law, in so far as this can be reconstructed. An examination of this question is justified, for if the "courtroom" analogy is pressed too far, it may be concluded that, just as in the ordinary courts an individual was convicted for a breach of the law, so in the prophetic lawsuit, Israel is indicted because she has broken specific stipulations contained in ancient Israel's legal codes /60/. It may be expedient here to include Is. 3:13-15 in our discussion, for it is generally recognised that the form of these verses is largely juristic in character, and some commentators have suggested that this passage was in fact based on the legal proceedings in the normal court of law /61/. Although the precise delimitation of the unit is uncertain, it will be assumed in the following discussion that the passage consists only of vv.13-15 /62/. The verses may be translated as follows:

13. The Lord stands up to plead,
        he stands to judge his people.[a]
14. The Lord enters into judgement
        with the elders and princes of his people:
    "You have devoured the vineyard,
        the spoil of the poor is in your houses.
15. What do you mean by crushing my people,
        and grinding the face of the poor?"
    says the Lord God of hosts.
a. It is probable that MT עמים should be emended to עמי

(cf. LXX, Syr.), since the judgement that follows indicates an indictment of Yahweh's own people, and not of the nations in general (Fohrer, Kaiser, Wildberger).

Before proceeding with our investigation, however, it is necessary to explain the methodology which will be employed in the following discussion, for the first problem that must be resolved is that of determining the nature of the ordinary judicial proceedings in ancient Israel. Unfortunately, the legislative codes of the Old Testament provide very little information on this issue, and consequently it is often assumed that the process of a trial in the normal court of law can be reconstructed by utilising various passages (such as those in Deutero-Isaiah and in the book of Job) which represent Yahweh's dispute with men as a formal trial. Köhler, for example, claimed that the use of the "lawsuits" in Deutero-Isaiah could provide information about the proceedings of a lawcourt in ancient Israel and about the legal terminology employed therein /63/. However, this method must be relinquished for the purpose of our investigation, for since both passages under discussion (Is. 1:2-3; 3:13-15) are commonly regarded as "lawsuits", such a method would here inevitably lead to circular arguments. Moreover, it is questionable whether any reliable deductions can be made concerning the normal process of law on the basis of various allusions in the poetic passages contained in the Old Testament. Thus, for example, it must not be assumed from Is. 3:13b, where it is stated that Yahweh stands to judge his people, that in the ordinary court the judge "stood" in order to pronounce the sentence /64/, for this would seem to be contradicted by other poetic passages (e.g. Ps. 9:5; Joel 4:12) where Yahweh is represented as "sitting" (presumably upon his heavenly throne) in order to pass judgement. The poetic texts cannot, therefore, be regarded as reliable guides to reconstruct the procedure which normally took place in the legal assembly, and it seems safer to draw conclusions from the narrative texts in the Old Testament which describe everyday legal proceedings (cf. 1 Kings 3:16ff.; 21:8ff.; Jer. 26:1ff.; Ruth 4:1ff.). From these texts, it appears that the general practice was for the plaintiff to call upon his witness and then to bring his accusation against the other party; if this party was unable to refute the accusation, then the sentence was announced and the judgement was passed /65/. It will be our concern in the discussion that follows to trace the extent to which the normal

II Israel's Rebellion Against Yahweh (Is. 1:2-3)

judicial procedure in Israel is reflected in the oracles contained in Is. 1:2-3; 3:13-15.

1. The Prophetic Lawsuit and Court Procedure
a. Yahweh as Plaintiff and Judge. It is assumed by many commentators that in Is. 1:2-3 Yahweh appears both as the plaintiff who brings an accusation against the people and as the judge who pronounces the sentence /66/. This dual role of plaintiff and judge is said to be apparent also in Is. 3:13-15, for here Yahweh, in his capacity as a plaintiff, accuses the officials and the leaders of the people of neglecting their responsibility, and in his capacity as a judge, he vindicates the cause of the poor against their oppressors /67/. Is there, therefore, any evidence to suggest the blurring of the roles of plaintiff and judge in the narrative portions of the Old Testament which describe legal procedures? A cursory glance at the relevant passages (1 Kings 3:16ff.; 21:8ff.; Jer. 26:1ff.; Ruth 4:1ff.) reveals a negative answer. This, of course, is hardly surprising, for no human court would have tolerated the impropriety of a man acting as judge in his own cause. Such a confusion of the roles of plaintiff and judge would have undermined the whole judicial process and would have destroyed the validity of the legal trial. It must be concluded, therefore, that if the plaintiff and judge are identified in Is. 1:2-3 and 3:13-15, then this particular feature finds no counterpart in the ordinary judicial procedure in Israel and Judah /68/.

b. Witnesses. The importance of witnesses in the normal legal trial in ancient Israel is attested by several passages in the Old Testament. Two witnesses are called upon in the trial of Naboth, and it is they who bring the accusation against him (1 Kings 21:8ff.). Similarly, when accusations are brought against Jeremiah, the plaintiff not only appeals to the facts of the case ("he has prophesied against this city") but he also finds it necessary to produce evidence ("as you have heard with your own ears"), and the purpose of this latter clause was presumably to establish witnesses for the offence (Jer. 26:11). In Israel, witnesses accepted responsibility for the sentence, and for this reason it was incumbent upon them to throw the first stone should the accused be found guilty (Deut. 17:7). The truth of the evidence cited by the witness was naturally a matter of great importance, and false witnesses were condemned to the punishment that would have befallen the accused (Deut. 19:18f.).

Having established the importance of the role of witnesses in the normal legal proceedings, we may now return to Is. 1:2-3; 3:13-15, and inquire whether there is any evidence that "witnesses" are called upon in these passages. Commentators who regard the invocation of "heaven and earth" in Is. 1:2a as a summons for witnesses to be present either refer to the function of these cosmic elements in the treaties /69/, or else they conclude that the term "heaven" is synonymous with the expression "hosts of heaven" and that the word "earth" actually designates "the inhabitants of the earth" /70/.

However, it must be emphasised that Isaiah does not explicitly state that "heaven and earth" are here to appear as "witnesses" to hear Yahweh's accusation. Indeed, there is no indication in any of the prophetic lawsuits that "heaven and earth" were to function as "witnesses", and it is, perhaps, significant that some scholars regard the cosmic phenomena as "judges" rather than as "witnesses" in the dispute between Yahweh and his people /71/. Thus, Köhler's contention that the invocation of cosmic elements in such passages as Deut. 32:1; Is. 1:2; Mic. 6:2 may be regarded as a device designed to reflect the legal custom of summoning two witnesses to be present in the case of a capital offence (Num. 35:30; Deut. 17:6) is simply conjectural /72/. His argument is considerably weakened by the fact that in Jer. 2:12 - which is often regarded as part of a lawsuit - only the "heavens" are invoked, and they are certainly not called upon as "witnesses", but simply to be appalled and shocked at the outrageousness of Israel's sin.

It may also be relevant here to note that in only three passages in the Old Testament is it stated expressis verbis that "heaven and earth" are to function as witnesses (Deut. 4:26; 30:19; 31:28). In these contexts, "heaven and earth" are to testify to the fact that Israel had disobeyed the covenant, an act which would, in turn, bring the curses of the covenant into operation. Since it is generally recognised that the standard Near Eastern treaty pattern has influenced the form and vocabulary of Deuteronomy /73/, it is conceivable that the function of "heaven and earth" in these particular contexts is to be explained on the analogy of the function of the cosmic elements in the treaties where they are mentioned as witnesses to the treaty document /74/. On the other hand, it has already been indicated that the evidence is not decisive enough to warrant the assumption that Is. 1:2-3 is to be viewed against a covenantal or treaty background /75/, and consequently it cannot be assumed that the function of "heaven and earth" in these verses is to be explained by referring to the function of the cosmic elements in the vassal-treaties.

The most probable explanation of the invocation of "heaven and earth" in Is. 1:2a is that this form of address was simply a stylistic device designed to draw attention to the importance of the words that follow. In a similar way, Deutero-Isaiah calls upon the coastlands and the far nations to listen as he unfolds the plans and designs of Yahweh (Is. 41:1; 49:1), and Jeremiah summons the nations and the whole earth to hear what Yahweh has determined for his people (Jer. 6:18f.). There is a sense, therefore, in which earlier commentators were correct in assuming that the appeal to "heaven and earth" in the various biblical passages had no function other than as an audience to a solemn declaration /76/.

It should, perhaps, be added that even if "heaven and earth" were to be regarded as witnesses in Is. 1:2-3, it is still doubtful whether the passage would correspond to the normal court procedure in Israel, for it has been shown that when witnesses were summoned during a trial, they were called by the parties themselves, and not by a judge or any other court official /77/. On the other hand, the "courtroom" analogy of Is. 1:2-3 would necessitate the presupposition that it was the prophet acting as a court official (Gerichtsdiener) who called the attention of the cosmic elements to the indictment which was brought by Yahweh.

Further, it may be noted that there is no mention of "heaven and earth" or witnesses of any kind in Is. 3:13-15. This is surely surprising if the passage is supposed to reflect actual court procedure. It is sometimes claimed that the presence of "witnesses" was here unnecessary, for the fact that the spoil of the poor could be found in the houses of the elders and princes (Is. 3:14b) was in itself sufficient evidence to ensure a conviction /78/. However, this argument can hardly be regarded as conclusive, for Jer. 26:11 seems to indicate that even when evidence could be produced, it was still necessary for it to be corroborated by the testimony of witnesses. Thus although the presence of witnesses was an important element in the ordinary legal proceedings, there is no evidence to indicate that witnesses of any kind were present in either of the passages under discussion.

c. The Sentence. As has already been indicated, the procedure in the normal court of law was that the plaintiff brought an accusation against the other party, and if this party was unable to refute the truth of the accusation then a sentence was announced and a judgement was passed. However, if Is. 1:2-3 was modelled on the proceedings of an ordinary legal trial, it must surely be surprising that the proclamation of judgement is here lacking even though the basis of the accusation is established and the justness of the accuser cannot be denied. Wildberger suggests that an announcement of judgement would have been superfluous in this context, for the punishment that would overtake a rebellious son was stated in the law (Deut. 21:18-21), and this stipulation would have been familiar to Isaiah's audience /79/. However, it is by no means certain that Isaiah was here referring to the law of Deut. 21:18-21 /80/.

Further, it is significant that no judgement is announced in Is. 3:13-15, and here, also, commentators who accept the "court-room" analogy are forced to conclude that the verdict is omitted because there would have been no doubt in the minds of the people as to what form the divine judgement would take /81/. But again this argument seems unsatisfactory, because the exact nature of the offence which the elders and princes had perpetrated is too vague and imprecise for the judgement to have been self-evident /82/.

It must be concluded, therefore, that yet another essential feature of the normal court proceedings, namely the proclamation of judgement, finds no counterpart in Is. 1:2-3 or 3:13-15.

d. The Style of the Accusation-Speech. Boecker's investigation into the form of the "accusation-speeches" (Anklagerede) used in the ordinary legal assemblies has led him to two main conclusions. Negatively, it may be concluded that there was no fixed formula of accusation, since the nature of the offence varied from one case to another; positively, it may be inferred that the accused was always referred to in the third person (1 Kings 21:13; Jer. 26:11) /83/. The "accusation-speech" was therefore addressed to the court, and not to the accused person. On the basis of this observation, Boecker has argued that the "accusation" in Is. 1:2-3 - which is also formulated in the third person style - has been constructed to conform to the pattern prevalent in normal court procedure /84/.

However, it would be hazardous to draw any far-reaching conclusions on the basis of the form of the accusation employed in Is. 1:2-3, for the prophet's accusations are often couched in the third person form of address (cf. Is. 1:4, 23b; 3:16 etc.).

II Israel's Rebellion Against Yahweh (Is. 1:2-3)

Moreover, Boecker's contention that the style of Is. 1:2-3 may be designated as an "accusation-speech" is based on the presupposition that the words were intended by the prophet as an indictment, whereas in fact it is quite possible that Isaiah's words should be classified as a Klage rather than an Anklage, a plaint rather than a complaint /85/. Further, if Is. 1:2-3 was based on the style of the "accusation-speeches" in the normal court of law, it is surprising that the oracle lacks the atmosphere of "opposition" - the argument and the counter-argument - which would have been evident in the regular legal proceedings /86/. Finally, it may be observed that if the evidence cited by Boecker in favour of the third person style of address is accepted, this would seem to suggest that Is. 3:13-15 was not modelled on the proceedings of the law court, for here the rulers are addressed directly: "You (we'attem) have devoured the vineyard, the spoil of the poor is in your houses (bebātêkem)".

On the basis of the arguments presented above, therefore, it seems unlikely that the form of the indictment contained in Is. 1:2-3 was based on the pattern of the ordinary legal procedure in Israel. It may further be remarked that the "courtroom" analogy still presents difficulties even when elevated into the concept of a heavenly assembly which serves as a court of law /87/. According to this view, the prophet is seen as the one who could hear what transpired during the heavenly proceedings, since he was privy to the secrets of the divine council (cf. 1 Kings 22:15ff.; Is. 6:1ff.; Jer. 23:18ff.). Moreover, he is regarded as the one who had been appointed as an officer of the court to announce the verdict. G.E. Wright has interpreted Is. 1:2-3 against this background, and has claimed that in this context heaven and earth are addressed as members of the divine assembly /88/. However, it is by no means certain that these verses should be interpreted in this way. Huffmon, for example, has criticised Wright's contention on the grounds that there is no biblical or extra-biblical evidence for the supposition that natural elements such as heaven and earth had any place in the divine assembly /89/. Moreover, Wright himself admits that the concept of a heavenly assembly would have proved a great threat to Yahwism, for it not only presupposed the existence of other gods, but also closely resembled in many respects the "assemblies" of polytheism /90/. If this was so, then it is hardly conceivable that Isaiah - who so vehemently opposed foreign influences on the cult (cf. Is. 1:29-31) - would have used such an analogy knowing that it carried in its wake all types of pagan connotations.

Our rejection of the arguments which have been advanced in favour of interpreting Is. 1:2-3; 3:13-15 against the background of the legal proceedings in a normal court of law or in a heavenly assembly should not, however, be taken to imply that we accept instead a cultic provenance of the form which is thought to underlie these passages. The cultic origin of the Gerichtsrede has been suggested by E. Würthwein /91/. He notes that in certain psalms Yahweh manifests himself as a judge who passes sentence upon Israel and the nations (Ps. 50:1-6; 76:8-10; 96:11-13; 98:7-9). He further suggests that such language should not be taken as mere imagery, for in the cult Yahweh was regarded as present in a very real sense and his judgement would have been proclaimed by a cult-official who spoke in Yahweh's name /92/. Würthwein therefore claims that the prophetic lawsuit was rooted in the cult, and one of the passages which he cites in support of his conclusion is Is. 3:13-15, where Yahweh is represented as judging the nations (ᶜammîm, v.13b). This is said to reflect the cultic pattern echoed in some of the psalms, for here the prophet leads his audience to expect a judgement against Israel's enemies, but in fact turns to pass judgement upon the people of Judah themselves, or at least upon their rulers and representatives.

However, it is doubtful whether Würthwein's arguments for the cultic provenance of the prophetic lawsuit can be sustained. His arguments have been criticised by F. Hesse who observes that although Yahweh is represented in the cult as passing judgement upon the earth (ʾereṣ), the world (tēbēl), and the nations (ᶜammîm), there is no evidence in the psalms (with the exception of Ps. 50) to indicate a judgement of Yahweh upon Israel. On the contrary, the psalms which Würthwein cites were predominantly concerned with Israel's welfare (šālôm) /93/. In a similar vein, Westermann argued that it was unnecessary to posit a special origin in a cultic drama as the Sitz im Leben of the prophetic lawsuit, and he claimed that the fact that the word rîb did not occur at all in the psalms cited by Würthwein considerably weakened his argument /94/. Further, Westermann observed that there were no "accusation-speeches" by Yahweh in the psalms noted by Würthwein, and consequently the only common ground between these psalms and the prophetic texts lay in a similarity of ideas rather than in a similarity of form /95/. It therefore appears unlikely that the form of the prophetic Gerichtsrede was derived from the cult.

In the above discussion, we have been primarily concerned to examine the evidence which has been adduced in support of the view that the oracles contained in Is. 1:2-3 and 3:13-15 were based on the analogy of the normal court procedure in Israel, and we have argued that some of the elements which were regarded as most essential in the regular legal assemblies find no counterpart in these oracles. It may, of course, be objected that we have been too literal in our approach, and that the prophet, in formulating Yahweh's accusation against his people on the pattern of the ordinary tribunals, was not overly concerned about the niceties of legal procedure. Further, it may be argued that a certain amount of latitude must be allowed when dealing with poetic texts which merely appropriate legal imagery, for in such passages Yahweh might well appear as both plaintiff and judge, since he could transcend all limitations such as those which circumscribe human activities.

While these objections are not without a certain force, it must nevertheless be stated that certain questions inevitably arise as a result of our examination of the supposed "courtroom" analogy of Is. 1:2-3 and 3:13-15. Can we really assume that the identity of Yahweh as judge and plaintiff would have been so self-evident in these oracles that the prophet felt no need to explain the fact? Moreover, is it necessary to attribute to "heaven and earth" the role of witnesses in a legal proceeding? Further, did the prophet really see himself as acting in the capacity of a Gerichtsdiener in a trial? Our examination would seem to indicate that it is doubtful whether the words contained in Is. 1:2-3 and 3:13-15 were intended to conjure up a picture of a legal assembly. That which emerges from a literary analysis of these oracles by modern scholars is not necessarily the same as that which would have been conveyed to the minds of Judeans living in the eighth century B.C.

2. The Law of Deut. 21:18-21

It has been suggested by some commentators that Yahweh's accusation against Israel in Is. 1:2-3 is to be viewed against the legal background of Deut. 21:18-21 where stubborn and rebellious sons who had persistently disobeyed their parents were to be brought before the elders at the gate of the city and punished /96/. The prophet here emphasises that Yahweh had conferred upon the nation the privileges of sonship, and that Israel's response was to be expressed in terms of filial obedience. But Israel had rebelled against Yahweh's authority and disregarded his commands, and the people were therefore required to face the consequences of their conduct.

However, although it may be admitted that some similarity exists between the theme of Is. 1:2-3 and that of Deut. 21:18-21, certain considerations seem to militate against the view that Isaiah's words are to be understood in terms of this particular legal provision. In the first place, it may be noted that there is no linguistic similarity between the passages to suggest a connection between them, for the words used in Deuteronomy to describe the behaviour of the son are sôrēr ûmôreh, whereas Isaiah uses the verb pāšaᶜ. Moreover, the text of Deut. 21:18-21 presents certain problems, not the least of which is the fact that the words "glutton" and "drunkard" (zôlēl wᵉsōbēᵓ) are appended to the initial charge of stubbornness and rebellion. If these words are authentic, it may be that the punishment prescribed in Deut. 21:21 is for selfishness and greed, or for anti-social drinking habits, in which case the connection with the accusation in Is. 1:2-3 would be considerably weakened /97/. Further, it may be observed that the tone of Isaiah's words in this passage would seem to preclude a background in Deut. 21:18-21. In the Deuteronomic passage, the "father" is representative of power and authority, but in Is. 1:2-3 the emphasis is upon Yahweh's fatherly care, and the concept of discipline seems far removed from Isaiah's thought /98/.

Moreover, it is doubtful whether an appeal to this law would have added much force to Isaiah's indictment, for the idea of respect and honour towards one's parents was basically an emotional one and did not fit too easily into the compartment of authoritative regulation. In this regard, commentators have observed that in all probability the law of Deut. 21:18-21 was not often resorted to in practice /99/, and this in itself suggests a recognition of the fact that the discipline of a son was not generally regarded as a specifically legal issue. In any case, it should be noted that the concept of honouring parents was by no means confined to the realm of law, as is shown by the frequent exhortations in the book of Proverbs concerning this subject (cf. Prov. 19:18; 22:15; 23:13f.; 29:15, 17). Further, Eissfeldt has emphasised that the notion of respect towards parents was a common one outside Israel, since it was assumed everywhere in the ancient world that children should instinctively be submissive and obedient towards their parents, especially towards the old who were no longer able to care for themselves /100/.

Such considerations as these suggest that considerable caution should be exercised before assuming that the accusation levelled against Israel in Is. 1:2-3 should be understood in terms of the specific legal provision contained in Deut. 21:18-21.

C. The Wisdom Background

It will now be necessary to examine the view that Is. 1:2-3 is to be understood against a background in the wisdom tradition /101/. The main argument which has been advanced in favour of the wisdom background of these verses is the prophet's use of the "parable" of the ox and the ass, for the words "the ox knows its owner and the ass its master's stall" in v.3a are said to be a proverbial expression reflecting the thought of the wisdom teachers who often had recourse to the animal kingdom to draw analogies for their instruction /102/. The behaviour of such creatures as the badger (Prov. 30:26), the ant (Prov. 6:6ff.; 30:25), the locust (Prov. 30:27) and the lizard (Prov. 30:28) was often regarded by the wise as a salutary example for humans to follow. The wisdom literature shows an awareness of a basic order (Grundordnung) to which the animate and inanimate world were likewise subjected, and the behaviour of animals was regarded by the wisdom teachers as reflecting this order since their actions generally exhibited that which was natural and reasonable /103/. Thus Isaiah's reference to the behaviour of the ox and the ass was intended to highlight the fact that Israel was devoid of the natural instincts with which even dumb animals were endowed.

Further, Isaiah's use of the "father-son" analogy is also regarded as significant when interpreted against a background in the wisdom tradition, for in the wisdom literature of Egypt, Babylonia and Israel, the teacher was generally designated as the "father" and the pupil as his "son" /104/. Whedbee finds a parallel to Is. 1:2-3 in the wisdom text Ahiqar, and he cites (among other passages) the following example: "My son, I trained up thy stature like a cedar, but thou hast humbled me in my life, and hast made me drunken with thy wickedness". Whedbee claims that the pattern here is basically the same as in Is. 1:2b, for the teacher/father cites the benevolent acts which he has performed on behalf of his pupil/son, and contrasts this with the son's flagrant ingratitude and rebellion /105/.

However, it is doubtful whether these arguments are in themselves sufficient to indicate that a wisdom background underlies Isaiah's words. In the first place, the mere use of the "parable" of the ox and the ass can hardly be regarded as a decisive argument in favour of wisdom influence, for such literary devices as the parable may have been used by any speaker for the sake of rhetorical effectiveness, and the use of such a device would therefore have been too widespread for one to be able to locate it in any particular tradition. Further, it is doubtful whether the concept of a father instructing his son should necessarily be taken to indicate influence from the realm of wisdom, for the same idea is common in texts outside the wisdom literature (cf. Gen. 45:8; Ex. 12:26f.; Deut. 6:6f.; Ps. 78:2ff.). Moreover, in the book of Proverbs the "sons" are generally addressed directly and in the singular (cf. Prov. 1:8, 10; 2:1; 3:1, 11, 21 etc.), whereas in Is. 1:2b they are referred to in the third person and in the plural.

Finally it has been suggested that the use of the verbs yāda^c and bîn in Is. 1:3 points to a background in the wisdom literature /106/, but this seems unlikely, for both verbs also occur together in Is. 6:9 where no wisdom influence has been suggested. Von Loewenclau has argued that the verb rûm in Is. 1:2b also has its roots in the wisdom literature (cf. Prov. 4:8; 14:34) /107/, but this is based on her interpretation of the word as meaning "to exalt" or "to bring to a position of honour" in this context, but it is more likely that the verb here means simply "to rear" or "to bring up".

The above considerations, therefore, would seem to indicate that the evidence is not decisive enough to warrant the conclusion that Isaiah's words in Is. 1:2-3 are to be viewed against a background in the wisdom tradition.

Conclusion

In this chapter we have been concerned to examine the various traditions which have been thought to underlie the oracle contained in Is. 1:2-3. It was suggested by some scholars that this oracle should be understood within the framework of covenant and treaty, and that the vocabulary and motifs used by Isaiah in this context were ultimately derived from the

II Israel's Rebellion Against Yahweh (Is. 1:2-3)

vassal-treaties of the ancient Near East. This view naturally presupposes the existence of a widespread tradition of form and language which was used to express the relationship between the suzerain and his vassal, and that this tradition was accessible to Isaiah and had been appropriated by him as a means of expressing the relationship between Yahweh and Israel. The presence in the prophetic literature of motifs and vocabulary associated with the covenant and treaty was taken by some scholars to indicate that the prophets themselves appealed to the covenant as the basis of Yahweh's claim upon his people, and that their indictments were based on a neglect to comply with Yahweh's expressed will as revealed in the covenant established at Sinai. It is clear, therefore, that any attempt to understand the ethical rationale underlying Isaiah's indictment would have to take into account the view that the prophet was influenced in his language and imagery by the political treaties of the ancient Near East. Since Is. 1:2-3 is often regarded as reflecting the motifs and vocabulary prevalent in the treaties, this passage has provided a convenient focal point for the discussion contained in this chapter.

The arguments which have been advanced in favour of the covenantal or treaty background of Is. 1:2-3 are based on the presupposition that particular expressions and motifs recur with sufficient frequency in the treaties to enable one to identify a specific covenant vocabulary with reasonable certainty. It has been our concern, however, to show that the vocabulary used in Is. 1:2-3 is too general to warrant the assumption that the prophet was dependent upon the terminology employed in the vassal-treaties of the ancient world. Such notions as Israel's "rebellion" ($p\bar{a}\check{s}a^c$) against Yahweh, or her claim to "know" ($y\bar{a}da^c$) God could be satisfactorily explained in the context of Israel's own religious life and experience without reference to the treaties and diplomatic documents of the ancient Near East. Moreover, it was concluded that the use of the "father-son" metaphor by the prophet was not intended to convey the notion of Yahweh as a suzerain and Israel as his vassal. On the contrary, the use of familial imagery made possible a departure from the strictly legal and formal aspects of the covenant and treaty by stressing instead the need for a personal commitment of Israel to Yahweh and a living relationship of the people to him. On the basis of such considerations as these, it is doubtful whether Is. 1:2-3 is to be understood against the background of treaty and covenant.

Prophecy and Ethics

We have also been concerned to examine the arguments which have been advanced in favour of the view that the form of speech underlying Is. 1:2-3 and 3:13-15 was based on the legal proceedings at the town gate. We felt that such an examination was necessary before any conclusion can be drawn with regard to the basis of the ethical teaching of the prophet, for if Isaiah can be shown to have used the form of speech employed in the ordinary legal proceedings, it might be concluded that he was actually indicting Israel for a breach of a specific provision in the law. However, we have argued that some of the essential features of the ordinary legal assembly, in so far as these can be reconstructed from the narratives contained in the Old Testament, are not represented in either Is. 1:2-3 or 3:13-15. While an exact parallel to the normal court procedure should not, perhaps, be expected in passages of poetry where the dispute between Yahweh and his people is represented in the form of a legal trial, it is nevertheless reasonable to expect at least some features of the ordinary court procedure to be represented in the poetic passages in question. Since these features are conspicuously absent in Is. 1:2-3 and 3:13-15, these passages cannot be regarded as having been patterned after the legal proceedings "at the gate". Consequently, the "courtroom" analogy cannot be pressed to show that Israel was here being indicted for a breach of any specific stipulation in the law. We have discussed one legal provision which could conceivably have served as a model for Isaiah's accusation (Deut. 21:18-21), but it was argued that it is unlikely that Isaiah's words are to be viewed against the background of the Deuteronomic law.

We have also examined the possibility that Isaiah's words in Is. 1:2-3 were based on concepts derived from the wisdom tradition, and it was concluded that the evidence was not sufficient to indicate the influence of the forms of speech employed by the wise, since the motifs and vocabulary used by the prophet in this oracle are too broadly-based to enable one to locate them in any particular tradition.

Chapter Three
THE ACQUISITION OF LAND (Is. 5:8-10)

8. Woe to those who add house to house,
        who join field to field
    until there is no more room,
        and you are made to live alone
        in the midst of the land.
9. In my ears the Lord of hosts has sworn:[a]
    "Surely many houses shall become a desolation,
        large and beautiful houses, without inhabitant.
10. For ten acres of vineyard shall yield but one bath,
        and a homer of seed shall yield but an ephah".

a. The text is here defective (lit. "in my ears the Lord of
Hosts"), and the translation of the LXX ἠκουσθη γαρ εἰς τα
ὦτα κυριου suggests the reading: כי נשמע. However, this
verb is probably a mistake for נשבע , since the following
particle (אם-לא)is generally used to introduce an oath.

Introduction

Isaiah is here describing the precarious situation which must
have confronted every smallholder during the eighth century
B.C. The lengthy reigns of Jeroboam II in Israel and Uzziah in
Judah saw a marked change in the economic condition of the
country, and there can be no doubt that the rising monetary
economy was leading to a crisis among the small land-owners.
Since they could not always support themselves from their own
crops, they became increasingly dependent upon the wealthier
citizens of the community, and they, in turn, took advantage of
the plight of the poor in order to increase their own estates.
The specific methods used to obtain these possessions are not
stated, nor indeed does the prophet mention precisely who was
responsible for such deeds. However, it is usually assumed that
Isaiah was referring either to the creditors who foreclosed
mortgaged houses and fields before the owner was in a position
to redeem them, or else to the high officials of the royal
administration in Jerusalem who attempted to expand the
crown-land bestowed upon them by the king. In the following

discussion, both possibilities must be considered, along with the legal provisions that may conceivably underlie the prophet's indictment. Further, the argument that the accusation should be understood against a background in the wisdom tradition will be discussed, and finally, the contention that Isaiah's words are here dependent on certain passages in the prophecy of Amos will be examined.

A. The Legal Background

1. Foreclosure of Property by the Creditor

It is thought probable by many scholars that the plight of poor farmers in Israel and Judah was, to some extent, aggravated by the custom of usury which prevailed during the period of the monarchy /1/. The demands of the small land-owners were supplied by loans secured in kind or in money from the wealthy, and it is generally assumed that it was the exorbitant interest rates which were being charged by the lenders that endangered the situation of the borrower and led eventually to his enslavement /2/. In a small, agricultural community, credit facilities were of the utmost importance, and it was inevitable that the poor land-owners should occasionally have to borrow grain or money from their wealthy neighbours. The custom may have been to borrow such items as were necessary in the autumn with the undertaking to repay them when the harvest had been completed. However, the farmers were often reduced to poverty by crop-failure, and consequently they must have found it almost impossible to return the goods which they had borrowed /3/.

In such circumstances, it was possible to discharge an unpaid debt by self-enslavement (cf. Lev. 25:39; 1 Sam. 2:5), and some would probably have welcomed the protection and security which the master generally provided for his slaves. Thus, those who had been reduced to poverty would have been able to gain sustenance which they would otherwise have found unobtainable /4/. It was often the case, however, that the peasant was forced into servitude, for the creditor was legally entitled to take him and his family into bondage /5/. It seems significant in this regard that Elisha accepted as a matter of course the complaint of the widow whose two sons had been seized by the creditor, and it appears that there was nothing that the prophet could do to prevent him from exercising his right (2 Kings 4:1ff.). Similarly, in the complaints recorded in Neh. 5:2ff., where

66

farmers were unable to repay their debts and had been forced
to deliver their sons and daughters into bondage, there is no
indication at all that the creditors were acting in any way
contrary to the law.

It appears that the personal liability of the debtor extended
to all his possessions as well as to members of his household, for
the law presupposes that the creditor might also seize property
in order to compel the debtor to pay his due (cf. Ex. 22:25;
Deut. 24:6, 10-13, 17), and Hebrew legislation merely demanded
the adoption of a humane attitude when this right was
exercised. There can be no doubt that in Israel this procedure
was often accompanied by force and violence (cf. Ezek. 22:12),
and the right of the creditor to seize the person of the debtor
and his family may well have been much abused. But the fact
remains that the creditor was legally entitled to distrain the
defaulting debtor together with his property, and the law, by
imposing limitations on the powers of the creditor, was merely
seeking to prevent him from abusing his legitimate rights /6/.

However, the law did advocate one measure which was
intended to alleviate the plight of the borrower. This was the
provision prohibiting the creditor from charging any interest on
the loan (Ex. 22:24; Deut. 23:20f.; Lev. 25:35ff.) /7/. The taking
of interest was forbidden presumably because it was regarded
as a method of profiting from another man's adversity, for the
loans in question would usually have been for the relief of
poverty brought about by misfortune or debt /8/. By prohibiting
the creditor from charging any interest rates, the law sought to
help the borrower by preventing the insolvency which was so
often the cause of his enslavement /9/.

It is possible, however, that these laws had certain
repercussions which had not been forseen by the legislator.
While the laws were clearly intended to favour the poorer
classes in society, they may, in fact, have served badly the
interests of those whom they were designed to protect. If the
creditor had no incentive to supply the money or goods needed
by the small land-owners, it may have been extremely difficult
for the latter to obtain a loan when faced with possible
impoverishment, and consequently those who would have been
most in need of some device by which they could borrow money
would probably have been unable to find willing lenders /10/. It
is hardly surprising, therefore, that the law found it necessary
to condemn the denial of a loan (Deut. 15:9), for if the exaction
of interest was prohibited, it is understandable that potential

creditors may have been reluctant to lend money to those in need /11/.

Naturally, the prohibition against usury does not necessarily mean that the law was always observed, and indeed there is evidence to indicate that money-lending at interest did, in fact, take place in Israel (cf. Ps. 15:5; Prov. 28:8; Ezek. 18:8) /12/. Yet, it seems significant that the eighth-century prophets, who were so preoccupied with the various ways in which the poor were being exploited and oppressed in Israel, never seem to refer to exorbitant interest rates as one of the underlying causes of the grievances suffered by the weaker members of the community. This has been taken to suggest that there was at least some degree of compliance with the laws prohibiting usury /13/. It is also noteworthy in this regard that nowhere in the Old Testament is there any reference either to the rate of interest which was charged in Israel or to the period over which interest was to be paid /14/. It is possible, therefore, that the creditors of Isaiah's day had designed other methods of deriving benefit from their loans - methods which would have provided them with an incentive to lend money without resorting to the prohibited practice of usury.

One such method may simply have involved the acceptance of a pledge. Although loans at interest to fellow-Israelites were forbidden, the law did permit the creditor to take from the borrower some form of security in the form of a pledge /15/. The retaining of such a pledge would therefore have been quite legal, and may indeed have proved profitable if it consisted of the land of the debtor or a member of his family. Although the creditor could never realise the value of the pledge by sale or exchange for the purpose of satisfying his claim, there is nothing to suggest that he could not use it to his own advantage /16/. Thus, under this system, the pledge may have served not merely as a guarantee of repayment, but also as a mode of satisfaction for the creditor who was able to utilise the pledge in order to recover his capital outlay /17/.

That such a commodity as land may occasionally have been taken over in pledge is shown by the incident recorded in Neh. 5:11ff., for this narrative describes a situation where sons and daughters who were in bondage could not be redeemed by their parents because their fields and vineyards had been forfeited (Neh. 5:5). When, as in this case, property was taken over in pledge, the creditor would have been able to enjoy the use of the land; such usufruct may not only have provided the interest on the loan but may also have contributed to the gradual amortisation of the debt. By retaining the pledge deposited by the borrower and using it to his own advantage, the creditor would have been able to mitigate the potential risk involved in lending his money or goods to the poor farmer.

It is possible that this custom, whereby the creditor could never become the actual owner of the pledge but could nevertheless utilise it for his own purpose, was adopted in Israel as a means to circumvent the law regarding the inalienability of property (Lev. 25:23). The basic principle underlying this law was that all property belonged to Yahweh and could not, therefore, be bought or sold at will. However, property given as a pledge could not be regarded as having been "alienated" in the strict sense of the term, since the creditor could never become its possessor, and the pledge, therefore, always remained redeemable /18/.

It is clear, therefore, that there existed methods by which land could be appropriated without transgressing the legal provisions safeguarding the rights of the individual to his patrimony. It is noticeable that Isaiah does not suggest that the means employed by the wealthy to acquire the property of others were in any way illegal, and it is possible that the methods adopted were not acts of open violence but devices which were within the limits of the law. If this was the case, then the smallholders could not have resorted to any legal tribunal to defend their claims, for the right of the creditor to seize the defaulting debtor together with his family and property had, in fact, been sanctioned by the law.

It must be noted, however, that the law did provide various means by which an impoverished farmer who had been reduced to bondage, or who had been compelled to surrender his patrimony to the creditor, might regain his freedom and his inheritance. The provision of redemption by the next-of-kin (Lev. 25:25), and the laws regarding the Sabbath year and the Jubilee (Deut. 15:1ff.; Lev. 25:8ff.) must be mentioned here, for they were all designed to relieve those whom misfortune had reduced to poverty, and to prevent the accumulation of immoderate wealth in the hands of a few. Since these laws present some problems of interpretation, it will be necessary to discuss them in more detail.

a. Redemption of Land by the Kinsman
The law provided that if a person had been forced through

poverty to sell his land, the next-of-kin had the right - and indeed the duty - to redeem that which his relative had sold, thus keeping the family property intact (Lev. 25:25-8). It is not certain whether the kinsman, after exercising his right of redemption, returned the property to the impoverished debtor or kept the land himself. Two factors may be adduced in favour of the former view. In the first place, the provision would be consistent with the other enactments of Lev. 25:25-8, where the land returns to the original owner either through self-purchase or through the Jubilee. Moreover, when the law refers to the redemption of a <u>person</u> from being the slave of the creditor (cf. Lev. 25:47ff.), it does not follow that he became the slave of the redeemer, for the purpose of the redemption was that he should gain his freedom and independence. Despite these arguments, however, it seems more probable that the redeemer retained the land in his own possession, at least until the year of the Jubilee, when it would presumably have reverted to its original owner. The purpose underlying the redemption of property - namely the retention of land within the tribe and family - would have been accomplished just as effectively in this way, especially since the original owner had shown himself to be incapable of maintaining the land. That the redeemer did, in fact, expect to keep the field in his own possession is clear from Jer. 32:6ff., where the prophet is depicted as paying seventeen shekels of silver to redeem the property of his cousin in order to keep the land in his own possession.

Although some families may have been saved from destitution by means of the law of redemption, it may be doubted whether this provision was always an effective method of alleviating the situation of the impoverished farmer who had sold his land. In the first place, it is clear that the debtor could be saved only if the redeemer was a wealthy person and was willing to fulfil his social obligation /19/. In those cases where a farmer belonged to a small family who possessed neither wealth nor influence, it is probable that the duty of redeeming the land would not have been performed. Moreover, the law could not force a reluctant kinsman to redeem his relative's property, and consequently it could not have been difficult for him to escape his obligation (cf. Ruth 3:13). The law did, in fact, contemplate a situation where an impoverished person had no redeemer to act on his behalf, and in such cases it provided that the owner himself might be entitled to repurchase his property if he later acquired the means of doing so (Lev. 25:26f.) /20/. However, this would seldom have taken place, for once a debtor was ruined to such an extent that he had to surrender his land and forego his liberty, the chances of his recovering on his own must have been slender.

b. The Sabbath Year

As has already been indicated, insolvency was one of the prime factors which led to the alienation of family property in Israel, for the smallholder would often have found it necessary to borrow from his wealthier neighbours money or goods which he was unable to repay. The institution of the Sabbath year was designed to alleviate in various ways the plight of the borrower, for the law stipulated that in the seventh year all debts which had been incurred during the previous six years were to be cancelled (Deut. 15:1-3), and all who had been reduced to slavery were to be released (Deut. 15:12-18; Ex. 21:2-6). Moreover, the land was to lie fallow in the seventh year in order to provide sustenance for the poor and the wild beasts (Lev. 25:3-7; Ex. 23:10f.). It is clear, therefore, that the basic purpose of the institution was to restore equality among the citizens and to give a new opportunity to those families who had become so impoverished that they had lost their possessions and their liberty.

The provisions relating to the Sabbath year are probably to be dated at an early stage in Israel's history /21/, and there are indications in various passages in the Old Testament (cf., e.g., Jer. 34) /22/ and in extra-biblical sources /23/ to suggest that these provisions were, indeed, observed, at least during certain periods /24/. It will therefore be necessary to discuss these provisions in more detail, and to examine the extent to which the institution of the Sabbath year was able to provide an effective remedy to alleviate the plight of the poor and the destitute in the land.

i. Cancellation of Debts. One way in which the law sought to help the situation of the borrower was by prescribing that all the debts which he had incurred during the previous six years should be released (šmṭ) at the end of the seventh year (Deut. 15:1). The precise nature of the release is further explicated in Deut. 15:2, and the most natural interpretation of the text is that it refers to the creditor (lit. "owner of a loan from his hand"), and that the law is here exhorting him to cancel (lit. "drop") that which he had loaned to his neighbour (cf. RSV) /25/. Whether this "release" (šᵉmiṭṭāh) entailed the complete cancellation of the debt or merely its temporary suspension is not entirely clear, but the logic underlying Deut. 15:9 would seem to favour the former possibility.

However, while this law was clearly designed to favour the borrower, it is possible that the effect of the šᵉmiṭṭāh was to harm the very classes which it sought to benefit, for many creditors may have used the approach of the Sabbath year as a pretext for refusing to grant a loan. Such a reaction on their part would have been quite understandable, for to lend something to a poor man in the sixth year would almost have been tantamount to giving him a gift. Indeed, the law itself envisaged a situation where, upon the approach of the seventh year, creditors would hesitate to make a loan if there was no hope that they would, in some way, be reimbursed (Deut. 15:9). Thus the effect of the šᵉmiṭṭāh may have been different from its original intention, and the law, which was designed to alleviate the plight of the borrower, could, in fact, have aggravated his situation by closing off all access to the credit facilities which were such an important factor in the agricultural community.

ii. Release of Slaves. Another element of which the Sabbath year was constituted was the release of all those who, during the previous six years, had been sold into slavery, or who had been forced by dire circumstances to sell themselves into bondage. This provision is found in Ex. 21:2-6 which stipulates that a Hebrew male slave was to serve a term of six years' servitude and was to be released in the seventh year /26/. It is probable that in this instance the six years were counted from the time a man entered into the service of his master. The Deuteronomic legislation (Deut. 15:12-18) extended the provision to include the emancipation of Hebrew female slaves, and it is probable that the legislator here intended a fixed year of release which would occur at the end of every seven years.

It is clear that the purpose of these laws was to relieve the situation of those whom misfortune had reduced to a position of dependence. Such laws, however, would not always have solved the problems of those who had been forced into a position of servitude. The situation of the slave after his release must have been very precarious, since he would seldom have had access to the resources necessary in order to establish himself as a free citizen in the community. The mere emancipation of a slave did not solve the problem of his rehabilitation, and the fact that the law found it necessary to exhort the master to furnish his slave with generous provisions upon his release (Deut. 15:13f.) is surely a recognition of this difficulty /27/. The slave, although subject to an obligation to observe certain constraints imposed upon him by his master, may often have preferred to remain in servitude than be set free and face the possibility of destitution /28/. It was not without reason, then, that the law permitted the slave to remain in bondage if he so wished (Ex. 21:5f.; Deut. 15:16f.), and it may well have been in his own interests to do so. It is clear, therefore, that the institution of the Sabbath year with its demand for the emancipation of Hebrew slaves after six years of servitude would not always have provided relief for the poor debtor who may have felt that his master could offer him the protection and support which he may have lacked had he been set free.

iii. The Fallow Year. The enactment of Ex. 23:10f. stipulates that the land was to be left fallow every seven years. Whether the primary intention was simply to avoid the total exhaustion of the soil /29/, or whether the provision was cultic in origin /30/ cannot be discussed here, but it is sufficient to note that the motive underlying the law as it is stated in Ex. 23:10f. was that the custom might benefit the poor amongst the people and the wild animals. It is not entirely clear whether the law of Ex. 23:10f. intended that the fallow be observed simultaneously throughout the land, or whether some system of rotation was to be used. The fact that the provision is placed in the Covenant Code alongside the Sabbath commandment (Ex. 23:12) might suggest that the custom was intended to be universal in its application. On the other hand, the fact that the purpose of the law was to provide sustenance for the poor and the wild animals suggests that the fallow must have been staggered by some system of rotation. There can be no doubt, however, that the fallow prescribed in Lev. 25:1-7, 20-2, was intended to apply to the whole country simultaneously.

This law would obviously have benefited, at least to some degree, the poor and the unpropertied citizens of the community. Although the fields had been left uncultivated, the poor would be allowed to eat everything that had grown of its own accord. The enactment would also have redounded to the advantage of many land-owners, for observance of this custom would have protected the fertility of the ground, and would have thus ensured a regular production in future years. However, it is conceivable that the law would have caused severe hardship to many smallholders in the land, for if they had been forced to borrow money or goods from their wealthier neighbours, they would inevitably, during a fallow year, have been less able than usual to meet their liabilities.

c. The Jubilee Year

The law of the Jubilee year, as recorded in Lev. 25:8ff., was a further provision which sought to restore the equilibrium in society by eliminating a practice whereby some accumulated much wealth while others remained totally dependent. The law provided that all land was to remain fallow, that all Israelite slaves were to be set free, and that each family be allowed to return to its ancestral estate. While it is clear that there was some degree of overlap between the provisions of the Jubilee and those of the Sabbath year, the distinctive feature of the former was undoubtedly the fact that all property, after a period of seven weeks of years, was to be restored to its original owner or to his descendants /31/. This was based on the principle that all land belonged ultimately to Yahweh and could not, therefore, be sold in perpetuity (Lev. 25:23). Since most people in Israel would have had some measure of economic independence if they owned a piece of land, the enactment of the Jubilee law simply sought to ensure the preservation of the economic basis on which the social order rested. The measures contained in the law of the Jubilee year were justified or sanctioned on theological grounds: the land could not be permanently alienated because it belonged to God (Lev. 25:23), and Israelites could not be sold into perpetual slavery because they were the servants of Yahweh who had redeemed them from Egypt (Lev. 25:39-42).

The chapter into which the law of the Jubilee year has been incorporated (Lev. 25) is generally regarded as composite /32/, and it is probable that laws of varying levels of antiquity have here been juxtaposed. However, it is likely that the provision requiring the return of ancestral property to its original owner was an ancient principle, probably dating from the early period of Israel's Settlement /33/.

The intention of the law of the Jubilee year was clearly to provide the families who had been forced to forego their possessions and their liberty with another opportunity to re-establish their position in the community. However, as was the case with the Sabbath year, there are grounds here, too, for scepticism regarding the effectiveness of the law in alleviating the situation of the poor. Thus, for example, while the law

III The Acquisition of Land (Is. 5:8-10)

demanded the release of slaves in the fiftieth year, it did not attempt to take into account the difficulties which would have been involved in re-integrating them into society. This was a serious omission in the law, for it must have been extremely difficult for any family who had been reduced to a state of destitution to re-establish themselves and simply continue their existence as before. It has already been suggested that the release of the slave in the Sabbath year would not always have been welcomed by him, since he may have felt economically more secure under the full protection of his master than if he were free and at the mercy of the creditors. Similarly, the prospect of rehabilitation in the fiftieth year must have appeared as little consolation to those who lacked the support of a wealthy family. Moreover, if a man had been forced to sell himself into servitude shortly after a year of the Jubilee, he would have been unlikely to live to see his freedom at the next Jubilee year. In effect, therefore, the provision could only guarantee the debtor's sons an independent opportunity to prove their capability to retrieve the family fortune. Some may actually have succeeded in doing so, but there can be no doubt that the majority would have failed, for such a prolonged period of servitude would have constituted a disaster from which many could never have expected to recover.

The practical implementation of the Jubilee laws, however, must inevitably have caused certain problems. In the first place, there can be no doubt that the reversion of land to its original owner in the Jubilee year would have entailed a great upheaval, for it meant that vast amounts of property would suddenly have changed hands at the same time, and this must have caused repercussions in practically every sphere of human life. Moreover, if the Jubilee occurred in the fiftieth year, as opposed to the seventh Sabbath year, the provision would almost certainly have proved to be economically disastrous, for the land would have been left fallow for two consecutive years.

On the basis of such considerations as these, some scholars have argued that the institution of the Jubilee was no more than an idealistic proposal which was never actually enforced in Israel /34/. However, this seems unlikely, and the existence of similar institutions elsewhere in the ancient Near East suggests that the Jubilee law was not simply an Utopian concept which was never realised /35/. Yet, it must be admitted that there is no evidence to indicate that the law was ever applied in Israel on a regular basis, although some scholars have maintained that

75

traces of the institution can be found in certain passages of the Old Testament /36/. It is, perhaps, also significant that there is no allusion to the Jubilee in either the Covenant Code or in Deuteronomy or, indeed, in the prophecies of Isaiah and Micah, both of whom denounced the accumulation of land (Is. 5:8-10; Mic. 2:1-5), and in whose oracles a reference to the Jubilee law might have been expected. This silence may indicate that the law of the Jubilee year had fallen into desuetude at a comparatively early stage, partly because of the difficulties involved in implementing the custom, and partly because the law, even when it had been put into effect, had failed to provide for the enslaved family a sustained and substantive recovery from such a period of prolonged recession.

2. Forfeiture of Land to the State

There can be no doubt that the establishment of the monarchy in Israel had made the country an important political factor, and it had also succeeded in creating the necessary conditions for considerable economic progress /37/. The king himself engaged in various commercial and industrial enterprises, and his demand for property would have been a necessary prerequisite for the effective continuance of the institution of the monarchy. Indeed, even before the appearance of the first king, Samuel had mentioned among the constitutional rights of the monarch the possibility of confiscating private lands and giving them to the king's servants (1 Sam. 8:14) /38/. Consequently, it is not surprising to find that the kings of Israel and Judah were owners of large estates (cf. 2 Sam. 14:30; 2 Chron. 26:6ff.), and some of the revenue from this property was probably used for the upkeep of the royal household. In fact, it appears that the king possessed sufficient land to be able to grant some of it not only to the members of his own family, but also to the high state officials, perhaps on the condition that the recipient of the fief perform certain services to the crown /39/. The narrative contained in 1 Sam. 17 may be instructive in this regard, for here it is stated that in return for slaying the king's enemy the hero is to be enriched by the king who will make his household ḥopšî in Israel, presumably with a fief of land which could be passed down from father to son (1 Sam. 17:25) /40/.

Inasmuch as crown-lands were bestowed upon certain individuals, it seems that they, as a result, derived their livelihood from the State and in return they were expected to render loyal service to the king and send some of the produce of their estate to the royal palace. In this regard, it is interesting to note that the Samaria ostraca, which are probably to be dated in the reigns of Jehoash and Jeroboam II /41/, suggest the existence in Israel of an administrative system in which servants of the king were supported by incomes derived from the royal estates. The typical formula on the ostraca reads: "In the tenth year: Sent from X to (l^e) Y: a jar of wine (or oil)" /42/. The fact that the ostraca were found in the government storehouse in Samaria suggests that the recipients were persons on official duty to the king. The most obvious interpretation of the ostraca is that they were bills of delivery accompanying shipments of wine and oil from the king's estates /43/. In a few cases, the deliveries went directly to the monarch, but for the most part, the recipients were probably royal officials and functionaries at the court of Samaria who held royal grants in connection with their services to the king.

Further evidence for the existence in Israel of crown-property may be found in the allusions in the Old Testament to the corvée or forced labour /44/. According to 1 Kings 5:27, it was Solomon who was the first to impose the corvée on all Israel, and he is said to have appointed Jeroboam "over all the forced labour of the house of Joseph" (1 Kings 11:28) /45/. But, in fact, the corvée was already in existence during David's reign (2 Sam. 12:31; 20:24; 1 Chron. 20:3), and the census which he imposed upon the people (2 Sam. 24:1ff.) probably had as one of its goals the registering of all those who were liable for compulsory service /46/. There can be no doubt, therefore, that the kings of Israel and Judah made use of the corvée as a means of securing unpaid labour for their building activities (1 Kings 9:15) as well as for work on the royal estates (1 Chron. 27:25-31; 2 Chron. 26:10; 32:27-9).

The evidence, therefore, would seem to indicate the existence of extensive crown property in Israel and Judah from the time of David and Solomon. Indeed, it appears that the royal estates had become so large that it became necessary for the king to appoint an official ^{ʾa}šer ^cal-habbayit (1 Kings 4:6; 16:9; 18:3; 2 Kings 10:5; 15:5; 18:18, 37; 19:2; Is. 22:15). The precise functions of this official are nowhere delineated in detail, but it is probable that his primary duty was to act as the administrator of the royal estate /47/.

But how did the kings of Israel and Judah come to possess so much property? One possibility is that dynastic changes contributed to the enlargement of the royal estate. The new king took over the former king's property (cf. 2 Sam. 9:7; 12:8) and much land may have accumulated in this way especially if - as was the case in the early period of the northern kingdom - there was a rapid succession of kings upon the throne /48/. Moreover, opportunities occasionally arose for the king to purchase land. Thus, David is said to have paid fifty shekels of silver for the threshing floor of Araunah (2 Sam. 24:24), and Omri bought the hill of Samaria from Shemer for two talents of silver (1 Kings 16:24) /49/. The accounts of these transactions, together with the fact that Ahab was willing to buy Naboth's vineyard or exchange it for another piece of land (1 Kings 21:2), suggest that there was no arbitrary dispossession of property on the part of the monarchy. On the contrary, the rules and regulations governing the acquisition of land in Israel were such that even the king could not transgress them with impunity.

Nevertheless, it seems that in Israel the monarchy did have a means of acquiring property beyond that which was warranted by the normal, customary procedure. Two narratives in the Old Testament seem instructive in this regard, for one suggests that the property of certain condemned criminals reverted automatically to the crown (1 Kings 21:1-16), while the other implies that any land which had been deserted for a prolonged period could be taken over by the king (2 Kings 8:1-6).

The narrative contained in 1 Kings 21:1-16 depicts Ahab's attempt to purchase a vineyard closely adjoining the palace of Jezreel. Naboth, however, refuses to sell his patrimonial inheritance and, as a result, Jezebel has him put on trial by arranging for two false witnesses to testify against him. The account indicates that the formalities of the law were obeyed to the letter. In the first place, Naboth's reply to Ahab ("The Lord forbid that I should give you the inheritance of my fathers") could easily be construed as blasphemy, and death by stoning was the penalty prescribed by the law for such an offence (1 Kings 21:3, 10; cf. Lev. 24:16). Further, in conformity with the requirement of the law, two witnesses were brought forward to give testimony (1 Kings 21:10; cf. Deut. 17:6; 19:15), and the fact that the execution of Naboth took place outside the walls of the city may similarly represent an attempt to observe the legal provisions which had been stipulated for the offence of blasphemy (1 Kings 21:13; cf. Lev. 24:14). Moreover, it has been suggested by some scholars that Ahab's attempt to "take possession" (yāraš; cf. 1 Kings 21:16, 18f.) of the vineyard

78

III The Acquisition of Land (Is. 5:8-10)

was not in itself a contravention of the law, but represented, rather, a legal act of royal confiscation whereby the property of criminals who had been found guilty of certain offences reverted immediately to the crown /50/. Thus, although the legal procedure as depicted in 1 Kings 21 was in itself corrupt, the narrative may nevertheless be taken to reflect a right which the king could legally exercise whenever certain criminals were condemned to the death penalty.

The other narrative, which is contained in 2 Kings 8:1-6, describes the plight of the Shunammite woman who, after a prolonged absence of seven years in the land of the Philistines, returned to find that her property had been taken over by the king. As a result of her appeal, however, the king ordered an official to restore the property to her and to make restitution for the produce of the seven years during which she had been absent (2 Kings 8:6).

On the basis of these two narratives, it may be inferred that the property of certain convicted criminals reverted automatically to the crown, as, indeed, did any land which had been abandoned by its owner for a prolonged period. These two methods of obtaining property must have been a continuous source of increase for the royal estates. Since there is nothing in either narrative to suggest that the king had appropriated the property in an illegal way, the possibility must remain open that there existed in Israel special rules and customs which applied only to the king /51/. It is conceivable, therefore, that there were legal stipulations governing royal property which were of a special character, as might befit the privileged position of its owner /52/.

But who was responsible for promulgating these new laws which had the effect of legalising the royal claim to property? One possibility that must be considered is that these stipulations were decreed by the king himself. There can be no doubt that the king in Israel did have certain legislative powers, although it is not always easy to determine exactly the extent and range of the judicial authority which he possessed /53/. While it is true that the historical books of the Old Testament never allude to the ability of the king to promulgate decrees, one case is recorded where David is depicted as issuing an order that the booty be shared between the combatants and those who had been left to guard the baggage. Although David was not king at the time, his decree is said to have become "a statute and an ordinance" for Israel (1 Sam. 30:24f.). Despite the paucity of evidence, therefore, it may be assumed that the king held legislative powers, at least in matters pertaining to the state, and it is probable that laws relating to taxation, military service and <u>corvée</u> labour would have been issued by royal order /54/.

However, although the king possessed the power to promulgate statutes, it seems unlikely that he would have been responsible for the new laws governing royal property in Israel. In this regard, Alt has drawn attention to the fact that the eighth-century prophets seldom addressed their indictments directly to the king; rather, their threats were levelled at the upper classes whose elevated position in society was due to their close association with the monarch /55/. If these were not actually relatives of the king, they would almost certainly have been his servants or his officials (cf. 2 Sam. 10:2; 13:31; 1 Kings 10:8; 2 Kings 14:5). According to Alt, it was to these wealthy and influential circles that the prophets directed their indictments, for these were the people primarily responsible for the gradual accumulation of property in the hands of the few /56/.

It is conceivable, therefore, that the new stipulations governing landed property were being drawn up by the king's officials in their attempt to expand the royal estate. However, since these officials stood in such a close relationship to the king, it may be taken for granted that in promulgating new statutes they did, in fact, have the full support of the monarch. On the other hand, it is unlikely that the king would have permitted the officials to disregard entirely the ancient order, for to have done so would have destroyed the very foundation upon which their authority depended /57/. The king could not have afforded a conflict on a vast scale with the old order, and it was important for the new institution to gain the confidence and support of the people at large. It was imperative, therefore, that the old laws remain valid, but that new stipulations be established which would take into account the change in the social structure and economic needs of the country. In this way, the "law of the king" (mišpaṭ hammelek) need not have replaced the old <u>Volksrecht,</u> for it was possible for both to exist in parallel. Thus, for example, the age-old rule that land could only be possessed by inheritance (<u>yāraš</u>) need not have been displaced; rather, the king's demand for land would simply have been couched in legal formulations which suggested that <u>his</u> claim to property was also a form of "inheritance", albeit an unorthodox one (cf. the use of yāraš in 1 Kings 21:16, 18f.). There is no need, therefore, to assume that the officials arbitrarily repealed laws that incorporated objectives of which they did not approve; on the contrary, these officials may well have persuaded themselves that they were not changing the ancient stipulations, but merely adapting them to the political exigencies of their age.

At this point, it may be expedient to discuss another passage in Isaiah where the prophet is evidently condemning those who devise inequitable laws (Is. 10:1-4) /58/. The text may be translated as follows:

1. Woe to those who decree unjust decrees,[a]
   and the writers who keep writing[b]
   oppression
2. that they may turn aside the needy from justice
   and rob the poor of my people
   of their right,
   that widows may become their spoil,
   and that they may plunder the orphans.
3. What will you do in the day of punishment
   and in the storm which will come from afar?
   To whom will you flee for help
   and where will you leave your riches?
4. Nothing remains but to crouch among the prisoners
   or fall among the slain.[c]
   In spite of all this his anger is not turned away
   and his hand is stretched out still.

a.   The form חקקי is unusual, and it occurs in only one other passage in the OT (Judg. 5:15). It is possible that IQIsa[a], which reads חוקקי, has preserved the original vocalisation (cf. G.R. Driver, "Hebrew Scrolls", JTS, N.S., ii, 1951, p.21).

b. The Pi‘el form of the root כתב occurs only here, and it was probably used to emphasise the zeal of those who continually wrote down iniquitous laws.

c. The text of v.4a is difficult, and the above translation, which follows that of the RSV, is simply an attempt to make sense of an ungrammatical construction. Lagarde (Symmicta, i, Göttingen, 1877, p.105) suggested emending MT בלתי כרע תחת אסיר to בלתי כרעת חת אסיר (Beltis is bowed down, Osiris is broken). However, this emendation must be rejected, for there is no evidence to suggest that

81

the worship of Egyptian deities was prevalent in Judah during the period of Isaiah's activity.

It has been suggested by Hentschke /59/ that Isaiah was here condemning a group of officials who held positions of some importance in society. Hentschke has subjected the terms ḥōq and ḥuqqāh to a detailed analysis, and has shown that in the pre-monarchial period, the meḥōqeqîm were those who held a prominent position among the leaders of the tribe. Further, the noun meḥōqēq in some early passages seems to refer to a rod of command, and it is possible that the chiefs of ancient Israel would have held the meḥōqēq in their hands as a symbol of their authority (cf. Gen. 49:10; Num. 21:18). Other texts, too, confirm the impression that the ḥōqēq was a man of some standing in the community (cf. Is. 33:22), and it is probable that the decrees (ḥuqqîm) which they issued could only be promulgated by those in a position of authority (cf. Gen. 47:26; 1 Sam. 30:24f.). Hence, there seems to be some justification for Hentschke's conclusion that those who were the object of Isaiah's rebuke in Is. 10:1ff. were, in fact, officials who had been given a prominent position in the life of the community and who used their authority to enact rules that would have been legally binding on those affected by them /60/.

That the decrees which these officials issued were in some way connected with the accumulation of land has been recognised by many commentators /61/. The phrase used by Isaiah to refer to these decrees was ḥiqqê-ʾāwen, and it is probable that the term ḥōq was taken originally from the procedure involving disputes concerning property, where the judge was asked to fix the boundary between neighbours (cf. Prov. 8:29; Mic. 7:11; Jer. 5:22) /62/. It has been suggested that in certain contexts there is implicit in the word ḥōq the notion of "right" or "privilege" (cf., e.g., Gen. 47:26) /63/. It is possible that a similar connotation should be attached to the word ḥōq as used in Is. 10:1, and that the statutes promulgated by the officials were designed to ensure that the king would receive that which was due to him.

It may be concluded, therefore, that those whom Isaiah condemned for devising iniquitous decrees were officers of standing in the community, and that the laws which they issued were connected with property, especially, perhaps, property to which the crown might have had some claim. Indeed, it is quite conceivable that the high officials who had been granted land by the king and who may have been the object of Isaiah's rebuke in Is. 5:8-10 were the very people who were responsible for the new stipulations which ensured that certain property reverted to the monarch. Thus the officials were, in effect, creating a legal basis for their own unscrupulous activities. It is natural to assume that the new laws were being enacted in the interests of the people who devised them, and among these people must be included the officials who had been granted land through the king's grace and favour. Thus, by issuing laws which were designed to ensure a continual supply of land to the king, they were, in effect, ensuring the continued existence of vast royal estates from which they themselves might hope to derive some benefit as a reward for their service and loyalty to the king.

B. The Wisdom Background

It will now be necessary to examine the possibility that Isaiah's condemnation of those who acquired the property of others should be seen against a background in the wisdom literature. This argument has been advanced in particular by J.W. Whedbee who observes that the unjust acquisition of land was the subject of many proverbs in biblical and extra-biblical wisdom texts /64/. The removal of the ancient landmark was strictly forbidden (cf. Prov. 23:10) and any attempt to rob the poor of his patrimony was strongly condemned (cf. Job 20:19).

However, the fact that the wise were concerned to protect the property of the poor in the community can hardly be regarded as decisive evidence for the wisdom background of Isaiah's oracle, for, as Whedbee himself admits, the unjust appropriation of property was a violation of ethical rules which would have been indigenous to any sedentary society, and consequently it is probable that the concern for property rights was too widespread to be limited to any particular tradition.

The possibility that Is. 5:8-10 is to be viewed against a background in the wisdom literature arises also from the prophet's use of the "woe-form", for it has been argued by some scholars, notably E. Gerstenberger /65/ and H.W. Wolff /66/, that the form derives ultimately from the wisdom of the clan (Sippenweisheit). An examination of the origin of the "woe-form" will, therefore, be necessary, for if the view advocated by these scholars can be sustained, it could be regarded as a strong argument in favour of understanding Isaiah's oracles in terms of ideas and expressions derived from the circle of the wise.

Wolff suggests that the appearance of the "woe-form" in Prov. 23:29f. supports his contention that the form derives ultimately from the wisdom literature. He notes that the woe is here followed by a plural participle and thus exhibits a similar form to the woe encountered in Am. 5:18f. Indeed, a similarity in content is also said to be apparent, for the passage in Proverbs is concerned to demonstrate the harmful effect of wine by comparing it to the experience of being bitten by a serpent, and Amos uses a similar analogy to depict the inevitability of judgement. Thus Wolff, while admitting that it is mistaken to think in terms of a dependence of one passage upon the other, nevertheless asserts that in both cases the same cultural background is presupposed /67/.

However, this argument is not as impressive as it may at first appear, for the word used in Prov. 23:29f. is not hôy but 'ôy. Wanke has rightly criticised Wolff for his failure to distinguish adequately between these two terms, and he emphasises that the difference in grammatical construction between hôy and 'ôy, together with the diversity of their distribution in the Old Testament, should warn against the identification of the one word with the other /68/. Hence, the fact that the word 'ôy occurs in the wisdom literature cannot be regarded as evidence for the wisdom provenance of hôy.

Wolff further appeals to the use in the Old Testament of the 'ašrê formula in support of his view of the wisdom background of the "woe-form", and he suggests that, just as in cultic terminology bārûk is opposed to 'ārûr, so in the clan, 'ašrê must have appeared as the natural antithesis to hôy /69/. Thus, if it could be demonstrated that the 'ašrê formula had its origin in the wisdom literature, and if this formula could be regarded as a genuine counterpart of the "woe-form", the possibility would arise that the term hôy itself derived from the circle of the wise. The evidence cited in support of the supposed antithetical relation of 'ašrê and hôy is twofold. First, two examples can actually be found in the Old Testament where the woe (hôy) and the blessing ('ašrê) appear in parallel (Eccles. 10:16f.; Is. 3:10f.), although emendation is necessary in both passages (reading hôy instead of 'î in the former, and 'ašrê instead of 'imrû in the latter). Secondly, the 'ašrê formula as used, for example, in Ps. 41:2 exhibits not only a similarity of form to that encountered in the prophetic woes (i.e. formula + participle), but also a similarity in content, for Ps. 41:2 deals with the care of the poor which is a predominant concern in the woes uttered by the prophets (cf. Is. 5:8ff.).

However, this argument must also be viewed with caution, for it is by no means certain that 'ašrê is to be regarded as the natural counterpart of hôy. The main argument against any close association between 'ašrê and hôy in the Old Testament lies in the distribution of these words, for the 'ašrê formula occurs predominantly in the Psalms, while the "woe-form" is confined almost exclusively to the prophetic literature. Further, the evidence furnished by Eccles. 10:16f. and Is. 3:10f. can hardly be regarded as decisive, for the most that these passages indicate is that hôy or 'ôy was regarded as one appropriate word which could be used as an antithesis of 'ašrê. Thus there is very little evidence to suggest that the term 'ašrê should be seen over against a negative counterpart, and even less to suggest that this counterpart must have been hôy. The fact remains that, in the great majority of cases, the term 'ašrê lacks an antithetical statement /70/.

The final argument adduced by Wolff is the fact that the woes of Hab. 2:6-19 are prefaced by the words māšāl, melîṣāh and ḥîdôt, and Wolff regards these terms as belonging primarily to the sphere of the wise /71/. However, this argument should be viewed with caution, for it is by no means certain that these words must be taken to indicate a background in the wisdom tradition. The word melîṣāh, for example, occurs only here and in Prov. 1:6, and consequently it would be somewhat precipitate to assume that the word belonged exclusively to the vocabulary of the wise. Further, it may be observed that the words māšāl and ḥîdôt are often found in passages outside the wisdom literature (cf. Judg. 14:12, 18; 1 Kings 10:1; Num. 23:7; 24:3; Deut. 28:37).

It must be regarded as doubtful, therefore, whether the term hôy was derived from the realm of wisdom, and it is not without significance that some scholars have argued that the original Sitz im Leben of the "woe-form" is to be found in the cult /72/ or in the funeral lament /73/. Although a detailed examination of the views of these scholars would transgress the limits of this chapter, some general observations concerning the attempts to trace the origin of the "woe-form" may be in order. In the first place, it must be observed that it is difficult to determine the extent to which particular forms are peculiar to one context, and were consciously borrowed from that context.

Thus, for example, even if it could be proved that the word hôy derived ultimately from the funeral lament, it is quite another step to argue that the prophets were themselves aware that the form was derived from this particular context, and that they intended the funerary connotation of the term to add force to their message concerning the end of Israel's existence. Moreover, it is questionable whether it is possible to posit any specific Sitz im Leben for what is, after all, only a grammatical construction. Thus to argue that the word hôy was used in the Sippenethos is not in itself sufficient to indicate the wisdom provenance of the term, for what must be demonstrated is that the term hôy became a distinctive formula which was confined to a distinctive realm where it acquired a distinctive predictability of occurrence and function. It may be concluded, therefore, that the various attempts to trace the origin of the word hôy are of limited value for our understanding of the term as used by the prophets, for the prophets themselves may have used the term on different occasions to express different sentiments.

To summarize: it is doubtful whether Isaiah's indictment of those who acquired the property of others is to be viewed against a background in the wisdom tradition. The condemnation of such a practice, while common in the wisdom literature, is too general and widespread to enable one to locate it in any particular tradition. Moreover, the evidence for the wisdom background of the word hôy cannot be regarded as convincing. The decisive argument against such a view is that the word hôy never occurs in the wisdom literature of the Old Testament, and even Gerstenberger admits that it is difficult to explain why more wisdom texts have not preserved this formula /74/.

C. Dependence on Amos

R. Fey has suggested that the words of Isaiah as recorded in Is. 5:8-10 exhibit a dependence on certain oracles uttered by his contemporary, Amos /75/. He notes that the unexpected occurrence in Is. 5:8-10 of the second person plural is a stylistic device which is reminiscent of Am. 5:11a, where a similar sudden transition is encountered. Moreover, the threat which is announced in Is. 5:9b to the effect that the luxurious houses will become desolate is regarded as an expanded version of similar statements found in Am. 3:15b and 6:11. Further, Fey maintains that the threat of a poor yield of crops found in Is. 5:10 is to be traced back to Am. 5:3. Finally, Fey suggests that Isaiah was here deliberately going beyond his Vorlage, for the addition of the words ᶜad 'epes māqôm in Is. 5:8 was intended to emphasise the extent to which the situation had reached in his own day.

However, it is doubtful whether these arguments are in themselves sufficient to demonstrate a dependence on the oracles of Amos. While it may be admitted that Amos condemns those who built houses of hewn stone and planted pleasant vineyards, he does not refer directly to those who deprived the landed peasantry of their estates. Further, while it is true that both prophets use the expression bāttîm rabbîm (Am. 3:15; Is. 5:9), this need not indicate a dependence on an Amos Vorlage, for the parallelism with the houses of ivory in Am. 3:15 would suggest that the expression here referred to the size of the dwellings in question ("great houses"; cf. RSV, NEB). It is only if this parallelism is ignored that the expression bāttîm rabbîm can be considered to mean "many houses", which is the obvious meaning of the phrase in Is. 5:9. Moreover, too much significance should not be attached to the fact that similar imagery is used in Am. 5:3 and Is. 5:10, for it is possible that the use of such imagery was simply the customary way of indicating that the impending destruction would be complete. Similarly, the fact that the punishment announced by both prophets is the same, namely that those who build luxurious houses and plant pleasant vineyards would not enjoy the fruits of their labour (Am. 3:15b; 6:11; Is. 5:9b), should not be taken to indicate a dependence of one prophet upon the other, since this may reflect a common phenomenon whereby the punishment is said to correspond to the crime (cf. Deut. 28:30; Mic. 6:15; Zeph. 1:13) /76/. Finally, Fey's attempt to explain the differences between the two prophets on the assumption that Isaiah was deliberately going beyond his Vorlage cannot be sustained, for this is simply a convenient way of explaining the presence of those features in Isaiah's oracles which have no counterpart in the oracles of his contemporary. On the basis of such considerations as these, therefore, Fey's interpretation of Is. 5:8-10 in terms of the influence of the utterances of Amos must be rejected.

Conclusion

In this chapter we have been concerned to examine the

traditions which have been thought to underlie Isaiah's indictment of those who sought to acquire the property of the poorer members of the community. In the first place, however, it was necessary to try to identify those who were guilty of perpetrating such deeds, and two possibilities were considered. One possibility was that Isaiah was referring to the creditors who were in a position to distrain the defaulting debtor together with his family and his property. It was emphasised that this practice was quite legal, since the creditor was allowed to take a pledge as a form of security, and this pledge may have consisted of the land of the debtor or a member of his family. The other possibility was that the prophet was referring to the royal officials who were attempting to expand the crown-land which had been granted them by the king. These officials were in a position to promulgate new decrees which had the effect of legalising the royal claim to property. However, in doing so, they were wise enough not to attempt to overrule entirely the old order. Nevertheless, under the changed circumstances, the new provisions could be justified and regarded as inevitable. By assuming the authority to enact such decrees, the officials were, in effect, creating a legal basis for their own unscrupulous activities. Thus whether Isaiah was condemning the creditors or the high officials of the royal administration in Jerusalem, it is clear that an appeal to any specific stipulation in the law would have had but little effect, for the methods adopted to acquire property were apparently not acts of open violence, but devices which could be brought within the limits of the law.

It has also been our concern in this chapter to examine the effectiveness of the laws designed to keep the land within the family and the laws designed to facilitate its recovery if lost. The provisions relating to the Sabbath year and the Jubilee were clearly important in this regard, for their basic purpose was to prevent the extremes of wealth and poverty and to hinder the development of an extensive latifundism. However, it was suggested that the effect of these provisions may have been different to the aim and intention of the law. Thus, for example, the law which demanded that in the Sabbath year the creditor was to give up his claim to whatever he had lent to his neighbour during the previous six years may appear to favour the situation of the borrower, but in reality the provision may have proved to be counter-productive, since it is conceivable that poor farmers would have had difficulty in finding willing lenders. The law also demanded the release of slaves in the seventh year, but this measure would not always have been effective in alleviating the plight of those who had been forced into a position of dependence, for a liberated slave without sufficient resources would inevitably have fallen back into the same state of servitude. In such a case, the cure may have proved worse than the disease, for the slave may have felt economically more secure under the protection of his master than if he were free and at the mercy of his creditors.

The law of the Jubilee year represented another attempt to preserve the independence of the smaller family units. The crucial factor underlying this provision - namely that all property belonged ultimately to Yahweh - meant that the rights of the human occupants were strictly limited. Thus land could not be bought or sold at will, and all property, after a period of seven weeks of years, had to return to its original owner or to his descendants. Despite this provision, however, it must have been extremely difficult for any family who had suffered a prolonged period of servitude to re-establish its position in the life of the community. Moreover, the implementation of the Jubilee law must have caused certain problems, for if the Jubilee occurred in the fiftieth year, as opposed to the seventh Sabbath year, this would have entailed two successive fallows, which would have been economically disastrous. It was suggested, therefore, that the Jubilee law fell into desuetude at a comparatively early period, partly because of the difficulties involved in its implementation, and partly because the law, even when it had been put into effect, had failed to provide an effective means of alleviating the position of those who had suffered a prolonged period of servitude.

In this chapter we have also been concerned to examine the possibility that Isaiah's indictment of those who acquired the property of others should be seen against a background in the wisdom tradition. It was observed, however, that concern for property rights was too widespread to enable one to limit it to any particular tradition, and that Isaiah's use of the word hôy could not be regarded as evidence for the wisdom background of his indictment. Finally, the arguments which have been advanced in favour of regarding Isaiah's words in terms of a dependence on the oracles of his contemporary, Amos, have been reviewed, and it was concluded that the arguments adduced by Fey fall short of demonstrating a dependence of one prophet upon the other.

Chapter Four

THE ADMINISTRATION OF JUSTICE (Is. 1:21-6)

21 How the faithful city
    has become a harlot!
She[a] was full of justice
    and righteousness lodged in her.[b]

22 Your silver has become dross,
    your liquor is adulterated.[c] [d]

23 Your princes are rebels
    and companions of thieves.
Every one loves a bribe
    and pursues after gifts.
They do not defend the orphan,
    and the cause of the widow does not come
    to them.

24 Therefore the Lord says,
    the Lord of hosts,
    the Mighty One of Israel:
"Ah, I will vent my wrath on my foes,
    and take vengeance upon my enemies.

25 I will turn my hand against you
    and will purify your dross as with lye[e]
    and remove all your alloy.

26 And I will restore your judges as at the
    first,
    and your counsellors as at the beginning.
Then you shall be called the city of
    righteousness,
    the faithful city".

a. Some commentators have suggested, on the basis of
the LXX, that the word ציון should be inserted before
מלאתי in v.21b (Kissane, Kaiser). But since MT yields a
tolerable sense as it stands, there is no need to emend the
text.

b. The words ועתה מרצחים are metrically superfluous
and have nothing to correspond to them in the first half of
the verse and it is probable, therefore, that they should be

deleted (so Duhm, Fohrer, Kaiser, Wildberger).

c.   BDB (p.554b) gives the verb מהל the meaning "to circumcise, weaken" (cf. מול "to circumcise"). The verb occurs only here in the OT, and it is probably to be understood figuratively in the sense of "mix" or "dilute" (cf. LXX μισγουσιν; Vulg. "mistum"). Other languages also speak of debasing liquids in similar terms (cf. the Latin "vinum castrare" and the French "couper du vin").

d.   The word במים is regarded as a later addition by some commentators, since it only expresses that which is self-evident (Duhm, Gray). The Versions, however, suggest that the word should here be retained.

e.   Many commentators regard כבר ("as with lye") as awkward in the present context, since elsewhere in the OT lye, an alkali, is only mentioned as a cleansing agent in washing (cf. Jer. 2:22; Mal. 3:2). Since the figure here is clearly that of refining metals, the word כבר is often emended to בכר "in the furnace" (e.g. Scott, Kaiser; cf. Prov. 17:3; 27:21; Is. 48:10). However, this emendation finds no support in the Versions and it is preferable to retain the reading of MT here, since there is evidence that alkali could sometimes be used as a flux to accelerate the process of purifying metals (cf. L. Köhler, "Sīg, sīgīm=Bleiglätte", ThZ, iii, 1947, pp.232-4). The meaning of the analogy would then be that Yahweh will purify Jerusalem as quickly and effectively as one might separate a metal from its ore by the use of alkali.

Introduction

The passage consists of a rebuke in the form of a lament over Jerusalem (vv.21-3) followed by a proclamation of judgement (vv.24-5) and a promise of restoration (v.26). These elements are constructed into a unity which effectively contrasts the present state of Jerusalem with the state of the city after Yahweh has restored it and purged the evil from its midst. The unit is constructed in such a way that the words of the prophet in vv.21-3 closely correspond to the words of Yahweh in vv.24-6 (v.21a = v.26b; v.21b = v.26a; v.22 = v.25; v.23 = v.24b) /1/. The date of the unit is uncertain, but it is probably to be placed in the early period of Isaiah's activity, since the content of v.23 resembles such passages as Is. 3:12-15; 5:22-4; 10:1-4 which are

91

usually regarded as early compositions /2/. The following verses (vv.27-8) continue the same theme, although commentators are almost unanimous in regarding these verses as a later addition, possibly dating from the exilic or post-exilic period /3/.

The passage will serve as a convenient basis for the following discussion of some of the problems concerned with the administration of justice in Israel. Those who suffered in the course of the legal trial were usually the weak and under-privileged members of the community, and it will be our concern in this chapter to examine the effectiveness of the laws which were designed to ensure their protection and support. It will also be necessary to examine the nature of the system by which they could appeal against an unjust decision rendered by the local assembly. Further, it will be argued that the injustice which they suffered was due not only to the corruption of the court officials but also to the way in which the legal assembly in Israel was constituted. Those who participated in the assembly "at the gate" were the elders of the community, and it is probable that these consisted of the senior male members of every household. Indeed, it would appear that the status of an "elder" was contingent upon possession of house and property, and if this was the case then it is clear that the legal assemblies could only have functioned properly while the citizens remained free, land-owning house-holders. Dispossession of property would therefore have entailed a loss of representation in the local assembly, and it is possible that Isaiah's concern for justice is to be directly related to his denunciation of those who evicted the poorer citizens from their small-holdings (Is. 5:8-10).

Similarly, it will be argued that the unenviable position of the widow in Israel was due to the fact that, in general, she possessed no property of her own. This was primarily due to the fact that the law provided no provision for the widow to inherit the estate of her deceased husband. If the widow had sons of her own, the estate would have passed automatically to them; if, on the other hand, the widow was childless, the property would have passed completely out of her hands, and she would have been compelled to rely on public charity for her support. Although the law sought to alleviate the position of the childless widow by allowing her brother-in-law or next-of-kin to take her in marriage and provide her with a son who would inherit the property of the deceased husband (Deut. 25:5-10), it would seem that this duty was not always performed by the levir and that he could easily have evaded his responsibility.

The chapter will conclude with a discussion of the wisdom background behind Isaiah's indictment, and with an examination of the theory that the prophet's concern with injustice and corruption is to be related to the similar concern found in the oracles of his contemporary, Amos.

A. The Legal Background

1. Bribery and Corruption

It appears from the indictments of the prophets that the acceptance of bribes was common in Israel, and it is probable that the courts were often no more than pliant instruments in the hands of the rich and powerful citizens of the community (cf. Is. 5:23; Mic. 3:11; Ezek. 22:12). It is not always clear from their accusations, however, whether the bribe was being offered by the litigant to the judge to decide cases in his favour or whether the bribe was offered to the witness as an inducement to distort the evidence in order to convict an innocent victim. In either case, the normal process of law would have been undermined and the justice due to the poor would consequently have been neglected.

Various laws were therefore designed to prevent such abuses in the operation of the legal system, and it is probable that the laws prohibiting the acceptance of bribes (Ex. 23:8; Deut. 16:19) were directed not only to the officers responsible for the administration of justice but to any citizen who might have had cause to participate in the legal assembly /4/. But how effective were these laws in preventing possible miscarriages of justice? The answer must depend to some degree on the status of the person to whom the bribe had been offered, for while the stipulations may have proved an adequate deterrent in preventing a witness from distorting the evidence, the same stipulations may have proved completely ineffectual in preventing the officials themselves from perverting the course of justice. If a witness had been bribed it is likely that, sooner or later, his perfidy would be discovered and that he would be punished accordingly. But the situation may have been different if the corruption had extended to the legal tribunal itself. The law would simply not have been enforced if those guilty of its infringement were the officials charged with its administration.

This is clearly an important factor to take into consideration if any adequate assessment is to be made of the legal basis underlying Isaiah's condemnation of bribery. The prophet twice mentions the acceptance of bribes (Is. 1:23; 5:23), and commentators have generally assumed that he is here appealing to the laws which prohibit venality in the lawcourts /5/. However, since it is likely that the recipients of the bribe in this instance were the court officials themselves rather than the witnesses (cf. the reference to the śārîm in Is. 1:23), it is questionable whether Isaiah was here appealing to any specific legal tradition. Appeal to the law would have served but little purpose, for in those cases where the judges were themselves guilty of judicial misconduct, the laws designed to prevent such abuses would simply not have been discharged.

It is possible that this particular infringement of the demands of legality may have tended to undermine men's confidence in, and respect for, the law generally. When justice was denied or denigrated in this way, the whole legal system must have been brought into disrepute.

We may conclude, then, that the laws designed to prohibit bribery were often rather limited in their effect. On the one hand, the law clearly recognised that an indispensable requirement for fairness in the court was that all the rules should be scrupulously observed by everyone who took part in the legal process, but on the other hand, problems would inevitably have arisen if the agencies of enforcement were themselves corrupt. The effectiveness of any law must have depended entirely on the presence of men of honesty and integrity who were willing to enforce it, and since such men were obviously lacking in the legal tribunals of Israel, little purpose would have been served by appealing to those stipulations which prohibited venality in the lawcourts.

2. The Right of Appeal

If the law was to be observed by those charged with its administration, it is obvious that some authority would have to possess the power to interfere with the local administration of justice whenever it was not being properly executed. In Israel, it would appear that this authority was vested in the king, for he held certain judicial powers and was regarded as the head of the judicial system /6/. The king occasionally acted as a judge (cf. 1 Kings 3:16-28), and it is likely that he functioned as a final arbiter in the difficult cases which the lesser authorities were unable to resolve. It is probable, too, that by making a direct appeal to him, redress could be obtained against a decision rendered by the local assembly. In this way, the king functioned not only as a judge in disputed cases but also as a kind of court of appeal /7/. In fact, the narrative recording Absalom's rebellion against David (2 Sam. 15:1-6) presupposes that at least at some time during the monarchical period there existed in Jerusalem a royal court of appeal to which every man in Israel could bring his complaint. Moreover, Solomon's palace is said to have contained a "porch of judgement" where the king could personally dispense justice (1 Kings 7:7). Any miscarriage of justice in the legal procedure "at the gate" could therefore be checked, since appeal could be made to a higher judicial body than the local assembly.

However, it seems that, in practice, certain defects were present in the machinery available for obtaining redress against the unjust decisions rendered by the local tribunals. In the first place, it is possible that in many cases the opportunity to appeal against the decision rendered by the local assembly would simply not arise, for if the punishment involved the death penalty this would have been carried out immediately by the witnesses present (cf. Deut. 21:18-21) /8/. Further, it is possible that the king himself might betray his office and neglect the responsibility of listening to the complaints of his subjects. In this regard, it is significant that Hosea found it necessary to remind the king that the correct administration of justice was ultimately his responsibility (Hos. 5:1f.) /9/. Moreover, the procedure available for appealing against the arbitrary decisions of the local assemblies was further undermined by the fact that the king was not always able to hear cases personally, and it is probable that he often had to delegate this responsibility to his officials. This measure would have been almost inevitable, for, if the corruption in the local assemblies was as prevalent as the prophetic oracles would seem to suggest, then the volume of appeals must have been quite appreciable. Indeed, it is probable that Absalom's attempt to gain the support of the people on the grounds that the king was not accessible to hear their complaints (cf. 2 Sam. 15:3) reflects a situation where grievances had accumulated to such a degree that the monarch was no longer able to hear all the appeals himself /10/.

It is not without significance, therefore, that when a court of appeal was later established at the central sanctuary in Jerusalem (Deut. 17:8ff.), the role of the king in the proceedings is not even mentioned, for the tribunal was presided over solely by the levitical priests and lay judges. Although the evidence is not explicit, it must be assumed that this tribunal replaced the right of appeal to the king or his deputy. However, it should be noted that there is no indication that the accused himself could appeal to this authority; rather, it was designed only for the benefit of the local assemblies who could refer to this tribunal certain difficult controversies which had been submitted to them for resolution /11/.

It seems, too, that a court of appeal was instituted by Jehoshaphat at Jerusalem (2 Chron. 19:4ff.) and that this court consisted of levites, priests and heads of families possessing supreme authority in cultic and civil matters /12/. In fact, the constitution of this tribunal is so similar to that of the court described in Deut. 17:8ff. that some scholars have doubted the historicity of the Chronicler's account of Jehoshaphat's judicial reform /13/. However, as Albright has shown, it is probable that the Chronicler's account of this event is, in the main, historically reliable /14/. The similarities and differences between the nature of the tribunal described in 2 Chron. 19:4ff. and that depicted in Deut. 17:8ff. may be satisfactorily accounted for by assuming that the Deuteronomic legislation arose out of the judicial reform of Jehoshaphat and represented in part a continuation and in part a modification of that reform /15/.

The judicial reorganisation instituted by Jehoshaphat seems to have involved the appointment of judges in all the fortified cities of Judah (2 Chron. 19:5). A. Phillips identifies these royal judges with the śārîm, for it is known that these were royally-appointed officials, and there is evidence to indicate that they were connected in some way with the administration of justice (cf. Is. 1:21ff.; Mic. 7:3; Jer. 26:10ff.) /16/. In addition, it is clear that these officers possessed authority in military matters /17/. The fact that the "judges" were appointed by Jehoshaphat specifically in the fortified cities of Judah is regarded as significant, for these were the cities in which soldiers were usually stationed, and the śārîm would therefore have been able to combine their military and judicial powers by relying on the support of the troops under their control to ensure that their judgements were enforced. Thus although Isaiah mentions the śārîm as responsible for the administration of justice in Jerusalem (Is. 1:21ff.), Phillips argues that it must not be concluded that these officers were confined to the capital; rather, they would have been found in all the fortified cities of Judah, since the śārîm were none other than the royal officials charged by Jehoshaphat to maintain justice in all the districts under their control.

This identification of the judges appointed by Jehoshaphat with the śārîm must be regarded as convincing, although it is doubtful whether Phillips is correct in maintaining that the appointment of these officials involved the abolition of the local jurisdiction of the elders /18/. Phillips recognises that the term "elder" (zāqēn) continued in use after Jehoshaphat's reform, but he suggests that the word in later contexts probably designated no more than "houseowner". However, it is unlikely that with the reorganisation the administration of justice passed completely out of the hands of the local elders, for as late as the time of Ezra the elders appear as a judicial body (Ezra 10:8), and they were clearly in a position to exercise judicial powers together with the judges (Ezra 10:14). It may be concluded, therefore, that the judges appointed by Jehoshaphat were the śārîm and that this institution existed alongside the ancient local jurisdiction of the elders.

There can be no doubt that the measures taken by Jehoshaphat were intended to relieve the king of some of his judicial responsibilities and also to provide a more adequate system than had existed hitherto to deal with the appeals against the decisions rendered by the local assembly. As has been indicated, the issues submitted to the king for his judicial decision would have been many and varied, and it is inconceivable that he would have been able to hear all the cases in person. Consequently, it was inevitable that this responsibility should be delegated to his officials, and this, in effect, was the outcome of Jehoshaphat's reform.

However, it is doubtful whether this measure proved an effective remedy to correct the abuses in the local administration of justice, for if the judges appointed by Jehoshaphat to deal with such matters were the śārîm, it is likely that the decision rendered by them was similarly influenced by monetary considerations. Little would have been gained, therefore, by appealing against an unfair decision to a higher authority, since the officers appointed by the king to listen to such complaints were themselves corrupt and willing to accept bribes (cf. Is. 1:21ff.; Mic. 7:3).

3. Laws Governing the Poor

Those who were most likely to suffer in the course of the

legal trial were the weak and underprivileged members of the community. The law, therefore, sought to eradicate every injustice by ensuring that rich and poor alike would be granted a fair hearing in the legal process, and stipulations were designed to ensure that the rights of the poor were not wrested from them by the more powerful and influential citizens. However, the law, in its concern for strict justice, also stipulated that the poor were not to be accorded special immunities on account of their poverty. This principle is clearly stated in the law contained in Ex. 23:3, which reads: "You shall not be partial to a poor man in his suit" (wedāl lōʾ tehdar berîbô). Many scholars have assumed that this verse is textually corrupt, since a court would hardly be tempted to favour a poor man who lacked both money and influence. Consequently, it has been suggested that wedāl should be emended to gādôl and that the verse should be translated: "You shall not be partial to a great man in his suit" /19/. However, this emendation is quite unnecessary, for the point of the law is simply that justice must in all circumstances be rendered with absolute impartiality. A judgement tainted by favouritism might constitute as much a threat to the legal system as a judgement perverted by corruption. It is no doubt a recognition of this fact which also lies behind the law of Lev. 19:15b, which stipulates: "You shall not favour the poor (dal) or be partial to the great (gādôl), but in righteousness shall you judge your neighbour" /20/.

Yet, it is conceivable that such stipulations as these, which require the application of the same law equally even to those who were not equal, may have been the cause of much hardship and distress. These laws, in effect, precluded the possibility of a judgement tempered by charity or clemency, and such enactments may have had the effect of leaving the judges free to apply the full rigour of the law to everyone whom they considered in need of being brought into line. Relatively minor infractions may have been burdened with severe penalties which could have threatened the offender with economic ruin. In this way, the law itself might become an instrument of injustice, and the legal process may have been undermined not simply through the corruption of officials but through a failure on their part to perceive the true nature of the problems involved and the consequences that might attend the severe penalties imposed.

It is possible that it is this failure which lies behind Micah's condemnation of the rulers of the house of Israel who, instead of executing justice, were prone to "tear the skin from the people and their flesh from their bones" (Mic. 3:2). There is no indication that the judges were here guilty of bribery or corruption; in fact, it is probable that nothing more discreditable was involved than a mechanical application of the same law to the rich and poor alike. The same may be true of Isaiah's condemnation of the elders and princes who devour the vineyards and take the spoil of the poor (Is. 3:13-15). Here, too, there is no indication that the judgements rendered by the tribunal had been perverted through bribery; yet, it is clear that their decisions could threaten the poor with economic oppression. It would appear, therefore, that in both cases the officials were condemned not because they had pronounced a dubious judgement or because they had indulged in doubtful interpretations of fact in rendering their decision, but simply because they had acted with somewhat more rigour than the occasion seemed to demand. The injustice against which the prophets inveighed may have been due to the failure of the judges to take into account the interests and needs of the individual litigants and their failure to exercise the freedom to interpret the law to fit the case at hand. The conduct of these officials may, in turn, have been justified by an appeal to the stipulation which stated that all men - irrespective of their social position or financial situation - were equally bound by the terms of the law and were therefore to be judged on an equal basis.

The assumption that the prophets, in their demand for justice (mišpāṭ), were merely calling for a stricter adherence to the basic principles of legality must, therefore, be viewed with some reserve, for it is possible that the application of such principles may have been the cause of many of the grievances suffered by the poor. The very rigidity with which certain laws were applied may have appeared to the prophets as more reprehensible than the activities which those laws sought to suppress. The concept of "equal justice for all" as enshrined in the law of Ex. 23:3 would not have appealed to the prophetic notion of "justice", for it is more likely that the prophets were advocates "d' une justice spéciale pour les pauvres et les faibles de la société" /21/. But even an apparently harsh law, such as that of Ex. 23:3, might serve a purpose as long as it was administered by a judge willing to mitigate its harshness in order to ensure a just verdict. The failure of the judges in this regard may have been the cause of many of the denunciations uttered by the prophets, for those who administered justice may have lacked the capacity for empathy which was necessary before any just decision could be rendered. It may be concluded, therefore, that the justice to which the prophets summoned men was no hard and unfeeling inflexibility, but a justice tempered by compassion and which reflected the divine compassion for Israel.

4. The Elders at the Gate

In Israel, ordinary cases were usually settled by a council of elders sitting at the gate of the town (cf. Deut. 21:19; Am. 5:10; Ps. 69:13) /22/. It is not certain on what basis the elders were selected for their office, but it has been suggested that the term z^{e}qēnîm refers to all males who had reached the age of puberty and who were capable of growing a beard (zāqān) /23/. The term "elders" would therefore embrace all the adult male citizens who played a part in the popular assembly /24/. But it seems more probable that the term "elder" did not denote every adult male citizen, but simply the senior male member of every household who would act as its spokesman in the affairs of the community /25/. This is suggested by the fact that the elders during the patriarchal period seem to have been the heads and representatives of the various families and clans /26/. Since this tribal and clan organisation persisted, to some degree, during the period of the monarchy, it is reasonable to suppose that those who were the elders of tribes and clans in the period prior to the Settlement later became the elders of the cities in which they subsequently resided /27/. This may explain the lack of any information concerning the way in which the elders in Israel were selected and authorised for their office, for their authority may have rested simply on the ancient tribal constitution. If this was the case, then it is clear that the term "elders" cannot be taken to refer to every adult male citizen in the community; nor, indeed, can the term be equated with the heads of only the most important families in a town or village. In the nomadic or semi-nomadic period every family had its clan-chieftain; it is likely therefore that, after the Settlement, every family had its elder who acted as its representative in the local assembly. The elders were therefore the male heads of every household, and it is not unlikely that ownership of house and property was a necessary requirement before a man could establish himself as an elder in the community /28/.

That the local assembly did, in fact, consist only of

propertied citizens may perhaps be confirmed by the description of the assembly contained in the account of Abraham's purchase of the cave and field of Machpelah given in Gen. 23:1ff. /29/. It appears from this narrative that the right to participate in the assembly was connected in some way with membership of the community, for the transaction is said to have been carried out in the presence of "all who went in at the gate of his city" (vv.10, 18), i.e. those who could be regarded as full citizens /30/. But it seems that this status was contingent upon possession of property, for it is clear that Abraham's lack of proper citizenship was due to the fact that, being merely a stranger and sojourner among them (v.4), he possessed no land of his own /31/. It was this lack which Abraham presumably attempted to correct by means of the negotiations /32/. Since participation in the assembly was virtually equated with membership of the community, and since such membership was granted only to those who possessed land of their own, it seems a reasonable inference that the assembly described in Gen. 23 consisted only of the propertied citizens of the district. Indeed, it is perhaps not without significance that these citizens are designated three times in the narrative as the "people of the land" (^{c}am-hā'āreṣ vv.7, 12f.).

Although the term "elder" is not actually used to designate those who participated in the assembly described in Gen. 23, the term zāqēn is used to designate the members of a very similar assembly described in Ruth 4:1ff. In both cases, the assembly takes place at the gate of the town /33/, and both narratives are concerned with a transaction involving property. Both assemblies were convened in order to witness the transfer of certain legal rights, and the question of rendering a judicial decision was not at issue. Since the nature and purpose of the assembly is so similar in both cases, it is possible that the qualification necessary to participate in the two assemblies was also similar. If this was the case, then possession of land would have been as important for the elders of Ruth 4 as it was for the citizens of Hebron in Gen. 23. The narrative concerning Abraham's purchase of the field and cave of Machpelah may then be taken to furnish some indirect support for the view that those who took part in the assemblies in Israel were the propertied citizens of the community.

It would seem, then, that as long as the citizens remained free, land-owning householders, they would have been entitled to participate in the local assembly, and in this way the general affairs of the community could be administered on a truly democratic basis, since each family would be represented in its deliberations. On the other hand, dispossession of land would have had dire consequences for every man and his family, for not only did it involve financial hardship but it would also have entailed a loss of representation in the local assembly. Thus Isaiah's condemnation of those who acquire the property of others (Is. 5:8-10) may be directly related to his passionate concern for justice in the assembly, since the judiciary could only function on a democratic basis as long as every man remained an independent, land-owning citizen. While he retained his own house and property he was entitled to assume the status of an elder, and his place in the legal assembly was assured. But if, for some reason, he was forced to sell his house and his estate, his status in the community was immediately reduced, and he would cease to enjoy the advantages of full citizenship. Having been deprived of his property, he would inevitably have been deprived of his rights in the community, and would no longer have been entitled to participate in the legal assembly /34/.

5. The Position of the Widow and Orphan

It is clear from the oracles of Isaiah that those who suffered the most in the legal assemblies were the widow and the orphan (Is. 1:17, 23; 10:1-4). While the paterfamilias was alive, the rights of his wife and children would have been protected since he, in his position as an elder in the community, would have been able to plead their cause before the legal assembly. However, when the husband died, the widow and her children would often have been quite defenceless and would have remained at the mercy of the community at large.

It is not surprising, therefore, that consideration for the widow and orphan is constantly enjoined in the Old Testament, and the law sought to legislate for their support by awarding them the privilege of gleaning the fields after the harvest (Lev. 19:9f.; 23:22; Deut. 24:19-22) and by ensuring that a triennial tithe be distributed among them to relieve their need (Deut. 14:28f.; 26:12-15). Moreover, oppression of the widow and orphan was strictly forbidden, and a severe punishment would overtake those who transgressed this provision (Ex. 22:20-3). In fact, this concern for the protection of the widow and orphan was a common phenomenon in the ancient Near East, and it is reflected in some of the oldest law codes. In the Sumerian code of Ur-Nammu, for example, the king declares that he had endeavoured to ensure that the widow and orphan were not oppressed by the wealthier and more powerful citizens of the community /35/, and in Babylonia, Hammurabi claims that under his rule the weak did not suffer oppression and the widow and orphan were given justice /36/.

Indeed, in the law codes of the ancient Near East, elaborate provisions were made to protect the widow by enabling her to inherit the property of her deceased husband. It is striking, however, that such provisions are conspicuously absent in Hebrew legislation, for here there was no provision permitting the wife of a man who had died childless to succeed to her husband's estate. The narrative included in Num. 27:1ff. is important in this regard, for it incorporates the inheritance scheme which prevailed at an early period in Israel's history /37/. The passage indicates that, upon the death of the father, the inheritance passed to the son, and in the absence of a son, a daughter was entitled to inherit the property; in default of daughters, however, the property passed to the brother of the deceased and, failing him, to the nearest male relative in the clan. Apart from the later development of inheritance by daughters, the order of inheritance was presumably the same as under the old custom /38/. The law would therefore seem to preclude the possibility of inheritance by the widow, for if she had children of her own, her deceased husband's estate passed to them, and if she had no children, the nearest kinsman of the husband would succeed to the estate.

The position of the widow who had sons of her own, however, must have been considerably more favourable than that of the childless widow, for although neither was entitled to inherit the property of the deceased husband, the widow with children could at least administer the estate on their behalf, and was therefore not without some measure of protection and support. But the plight of the childless widow was particularly distressing, since she would have lost all claims to her husband's estate.

It is not entirely clear whether the prophets, in their pleas for compassion towards the widow, are referring specifically to the childless widow or to the widow who had children of her own. The references to the "widow and orphan" (cf. Jer. 49:11; Ezek. 22:7) are somewhat ambiguous, for they may, on the one hand, refer to the widow and her child (taking yātôm to mean "fatherless" with RSV) or they may, on the other hand, refer to two distinct groups in society - the widow (whether childless or not) and the "orphan", i.e. the child who had lost both parents (cf. NEB). The term yātôm admits of both interpretations, for while the word could certainly be used to designate children whose father had died /39/, there is nothing to suggest that the same word could not be used to refer to a child who had lost his father and mother.

But whether the widow was childless or not, the fact remains that she herself had no claim on her husband's estate. This does not mean, however, that she could not possess property which she had acquired by other means (cf. Prov. 15:25). It is possible, for example, that the widow may have received property as a gift from her father on the occasion of her marriage (cf. Josh. 15:19; Judg. 1:15). Moreover, in the narrative recorded in 2 Kings 8:1ff., a widow seems to have possession of a certain amount of land. However, since this narrative indicates that the widow was not childless (vv.1, 5), it may be assumed that her son would eventually have inherited the property, and it is probable that she was simply administering the estate on his behalf until he would have been old enough to cultivate it himself. Naomi's possession of property (Ruth 4:1ff.) is more difficult to explain, for both her sons had died without leaving any progeny, and since she was now past child-bearing age (Ruth 1:11ff.) the possibility seems to be precluded that she, too, was merely holding the land in a fiduciary capacity until heirs were born who would inherit the land and administer it for themselves. How Naomi came to possess this land cannot be discussed here, but it is clear that a widow could, in certain circumstances, be found to be in possession of property even if this amounted to nothing more than administering the estate on a temporary basis until her sons were old enough to look after it themselves.

However, it must be emphasised that possession of property by a widow was almost certainly the exception rather than the rule. As has already been indicated, this was due to the fact that no provisions were made permitting the widow to inherit her husband's estate. In general, therefore, the widow was among the landless members of society and, as such, she is often mentioned along with the alien and the poor and commended to the mercy of the community at large. The provisions enabling widows to glean the fields and vineyards of others may be a recognition of the fact that they normally had no land of their own to cultivate. These laws, therefore, may represent an appeal to the benevolence of the property-owners to help the landless members of the community /40/.

But it is doubtful whether these provisions were adequate to alleviate the unfortunate position of the widow and orphan in society. The real cause of the widow's hardship stemmed from the fact that she owned no property of her own, and this was due largely to the absence of any legislation enabling her to inherit her husband's estate. Thus, not only was the widow deprived of a commodity which would have provided her with a source of security, but she was also deprived of a commodity which would have ensured her position in the life of the community. It is in this regard that the fundamental inadequacy of the laws legislating for her support comes most clearly into focus, for no amount of provisions enabling the widow to glean the fields and vineyards of others could ever make up for the loss of civil rights which befell those who possessed no land of their own.

The law did, however, make one provision which might enable a childless widow to benefit from the property of her deceased husband. This was the law known as levirate marriage which stipulated that, if a man had died without leaving progeny, the brothers of the deceased had the responsibility of providing the widow with male heirs (Deut. 25:5-10). On the one hand, this provision would have allowed the widow to reap at least some benefit from her husband's estate by providing her with a son who would inherit the property; on the other hand, marriage to the levir would have afforded her with some measure of protection and security, since he, in his capacity as a land-owning citizen, would have been entitled to represent the widow in the legal assembly.

However, it would appear that this provision was somewhat limited in its effect. In the first place, the provision was not clothed with any legal sanction; it was simply a rule which derived its only force from the general disapprobation falling upon those who transgressed it. The method employed to ensure that the duty was performed by the kinsman was not the imposition of legal penalties but simply the moral coercion of public opinion. Secondly, the disadvantages of performing the duty may often have outweighed the advantages, and in such cases the levir may have sought to evade his responsibility. Consequently, there must have been many cases of widowhood in Israel where the levirate did not occur and where the childless widow would have remained completely destitute and at the mercy of the community at large /41/.

B. The Wisdom Background

The wisdom background of Isaiah's oracles concerning the administration of justice in the legal assembly has been suggested for two reasons. In the first place, Isaiah's concern for the position of the poor and underprivileged in the assembly is said to reflect a similar concern exhibited in the wisdom literature of the Old Testament /42/. Secondly, his condemnation of bribery and corruption is said to have been influenced by ideas prevalent in wisdom circles /43/.

Whedbee points out that concern for the poor is a common theme in legal- and wisdom-traditions (cf. Lev. 19:13; Prov. 22:22f.), and he suggests that in Isaiah's indictments "the common roots of wisdom and law are highlighted" /44/. The legal background has been discussed in some detail above and need not concern us here. With regard to the wisdom background, it may be conceded that some passages in the book of Proverbs express a concern with the plight of the poor which is similar to that found in the oracles of Isaiah, but on the other hand it should also be noted that many other passages in Proverbs might be cited which exhibit an attitude that is in marked contrast to that generally found in the prophetic literature /45/. Often in the book of Proverbs there is a resigned acceptance of wealth and poverty as an inevitable part of the framework of human existence and, by and large, the wisdom writers - unlike the prophets - regard poverty and oppression as crosses to be borne and not as injustices to be remedied (cf. Prov. 22:2; 29:13). Moreover, the feelings of pity and compassion towards the poor which are so characteristic of Isaiah's oracles are conspicuously lacking in the wisdom texts. Indeed, in the wisdom literature, poverty is often viewed with some contempt and it is regarded as being due to intemperance and extravagance (Prov. 23:20f.), idleness (Prov. 10:4; 19:15; 20:4), squandered opportunities (Prov. 20:13) or the pursuit of vain pleasures (Prov. 12:11; 21:17) /46/. The prophets, on the other hand, have a more realistic outlook towards poverty, for they view it as a real social problem and one which was not necessarily the outcome of the moral failures of certain individuals.

It may also be noted here that although the wisdom literature of the Old Testament expresses concern for the plight of the widow and the orphan (Prov. 15:25; 23:10), there is not a single instance in the book of Proverbs where the widow and orphan are mentioned together /47/. This is surprising, especially in view of the frequent collocation of these terms elsewhere in the Old Testament.

H.W. Wolff has argued that Isaiah's condemnation of those who accept bribes should be seen against the background of court wisdom /48/. The difficulty with this view, however, is that although Hebrew wisdom extols impartiality in judgement and condemns the acceptance of gifts and bribes (cf. Prov. 15:27; 17:15, 23), its teaching on the subject is by no means consistent, for other proverbs could be cited which suggest that bribes could be justifiably employed in various circumstances as long as they produced the desired result (Prov. 17:8; 19:6; 21:14) /49/. Clearly, the wisdom writers, with their characteristically rational approach to life, were not prepared to ignore the undeniable facts of human experience. Here, as elsewhere, their counsel was pragmatic and motivated simply by an ethic of self-interest. But this ethic is surely difficult to reconcile with Isaiah's pronouncements concerning the acceptance of gifts and rewards, for the notion that bribery may, in certain circumstances, be efficacious is hardly a sentiment with which he would have concurred (cf. Is. 1:23; 5:23).

The wisdom background of Isaiah's indictment must therefore be rejected, for it simply fails to take into account the opposing philosophies which are encountered within the wisdom tradition itself. While Isaiah's oracles concerning the plight of the poor and the acceptance of bribes may find certain parallels in the wisdom literature, it must be emphasised that this genre also contains ideas and notions which would have been diametrically opposed to the teaching of the prophet.

C. Dependence on Amos

The possibility that Isaiah's concern with bribery and corruption is dependent on a similar concern exhibited in the oracles of Amos has been suggested by R. Fey /50/ on the basis of the linguistic and thematic affinities between Is. 5:20, 23 and Am. 5:7, 10, 12b. According to Fey, Isaiah's rebuke concerning the inversion of values (Is. 5:20) was suggested to him by the single word hahōp^{e}kîm in Am. 5:7a and by similar contrasts found elsewhere in Amos' teaching (cf. Am. 5:14, 18). Any differences between Amos and Isaiah in this respect may be accounted for by the attempt of the latter to sharpen the antithesis found in his Vorlage, and in doing so, Isaiah was able to attain a stylistic unity and rhetorical effectiveness of his own. Thus, for example, while Amos in his oracles intended the concept of "light and darkness" to be interpreted literally, Isaiah deliberately elevated this concept into the ethical sphere, for his concern was primarily with "deeds of darkness". Fey also maintains that the similarity between the two prophets arises from their use of the concepts of ṣᵉdāqāh and ṣaddîq, and from their reference to the acceptance of bribes.

However, it is doubtful whether such a dependence on the words of Amos can here be affirmed. Fey's argument is weakened by the fact that there is no evidence to suggest that Is. 5:23 should be transposed to follow Is. 5:20 in order to form a unit, and he himself is forced to concede that the reason for the present location of these verses in the Massoretic text cannot be explained. Moreover, the terms used by Isaiah in Is. 5:23, namely rāšāᶜ and ṣaddîq /51/, are common forensic terms used to designate the guilty and the innocent in a legal trial (cf. Ex. 23:7; Deut. 25:1). Similarly, in Am. 5:12b the ṣaddîq is the man who, during the legal procedure, is found to be in the right. Since the term ṣaddîq is simply a terminus technicus to designate an innocent man in the context of a legal trial, it is hardly surprising that the word should have been used by the two prophets and that it should have a similar connotation in both cases.

Moreover, while it is true that Amos and Isaiah advert to the acceptance of bribes, it must be emphasised that a different word is used in each case (šōḥad in Is. 5:23; kōper in Am. 5:12). Although both words are translated as "bribe" by the RSV, it is probable that some distinction should be drawn between them. The word šōḥad is generally used to refer to money given to a judge in order to influence his decision and secure an acquittal (cf. Ex. 23:8; 1 Sam. 8:3), although there is evidence that the term may also have been used in the wider context of making overtures of reconciliation by sending a gift or present (cf. 1 Kings 15:19; 2 Kings 16:8). The word kōper, on the other hand, was a general term for anything offered in lieu of punishment as a legal satisfaction (cf. Prov. 13:8; 21:18). The purpose of the payment of kōper was to restore the equilibrium between two parties which had been disturbed by the wrongful act of one of them. The punishment was assessed in monetary terms, and the amount of damages awarded would no doubt have been related quantitatively to the extent of the loss. However, the law makes it clear that not all offences could be cancelled by the payment of a pecuniary equivalent, and it expressly stipulates that no kōper could be paid for either a murderer or one guilty of manslaughter (Num. 35:31) /52/.

However, there is evidence to indicate that a kōper was occasionally accepted even in cases where the death penalty should have been imposed. One such case is described in Prov. 6:35, where an adulterer seeks to escape punishment by the payment of money to the injured husband. The law stated that the punishment for adultery was the death penalty (Deut. 22:22-4; Lev. 20:10), and it is this which the adulterer tries to avoid by the payment of compensation /53/. Although the text does not state who would have determined the amount of money to be paid, it is likely that this was the responsibility of the legal assembly, although it may have been arranged in consultation with the injured husband /54/. It is clear from Prov. 6:35, therefore, that an offence which would once have incurred the death penalty was, in a later period, expiated simply by the payment of a sum of money.

It is possible that Amos' condemnation of the legal assemblies for their acceptance of kōper was based on the fact that these authorities were now allowing more serious offences (such as murder) to be expiated by the payment of money instead of ensuring that the proper penalty for such offences be duly carried out /55/. In this way, the guilty, instead of incurring the death penalty, would simply have paid a sum of money to the relatives of the victim, and by their acceptance of this financial reparation, a mutual accomodation of interests would have been reached. The fact that Amos mentions the legal assemblies as accepting the payment in this instance may indicate that the money was originally paid to them and that they, in turn, would have rewarded the relatives of the injured party accordingly. It may be suggested, therefore, that what lies at the basis of Amos' indictment (Am. 5:12) is not simply the giving of a bribe in order to influence a decision, but rather the placid acceptance by the legal assemblies of monetary compensation for crimes which should have incurred the death penalty. If this interpretation is correct, then Fey's argument for a dependence of Isaiah upon Amos is further undermined, for the two prophets would have been concerned with two offences of a very different nature.

Conclusion

In this chapter, we have examined, first, the legal background behind Isaiah's indictment of those who administered justice in the legal assembly. It was suggested that the injustice prevalent in the assembly was partly due to the corruption of the court officials who were prepared to accept bribes as an inducement to render an unjust verdict. While it was possible, in theory, to appeal against such a decision by taking the matter before the king or his delegated official, this procedure would only have had a limited effect in correcting possible miscarriages of justice. In the first place, the king was often inaccessible and was unable to hear all the appeals in person; secondly, the officials to whom he had delegated the responsibility of hearing the cases (the śārîm) were themselves corrupt and would not always have rendered an equitable decision.

It was observed that those who were most likely to suffer such grievances were the poor and underprivileged who were often quite defenceless against the more powerful and influential citizens of the community. Although the law was regarded as being especially solicitous of the weak and defenceless, it nevertheless stipulated that one must not allow feelings of pity or compassion towards them to influence one's judgement. Thus, on the one hand, a command was given to execute justice to the weak (Ex. 23:6) and, on the other hand, the law warned against any tendency to favour the poor in spite of his guilt (Ex. 23:3). While this rule may appear to be harsh and unfair, we have seen that it need not contradict the basic purpose of the legal order, which was that justice must in all circumstances be rendered with absolute impartiality. It is not difficult, however, to see how such a law could have been abused by those charged with its administration, for it may have been interpreted in a narrow and restrictively literal manner by the imposition of heavy penalties for relatively minor infractions or by an insistence that every crime should be expiated in full, irrespective of the social or economic position of the defendant. It was suggested that some of the accusations of the prophets were directed against such narrow legalism and scrupulous literalism (cf. Mic. 3:1-3; Is. 3:13-5). Moreover, it was observed that caution must be exercised before any sweeping assessment of Isaiah's indictments in terms of a "legal background" is made, for it was possible that injustice might prevail in the assembly even when the prescribed rules were carried out with the greatest

110

exactitude.

It was also suggested that the injustice in the legal assembly may have been due to the way in which the assembly itself was constituted. Those who were entitled to participate in these assemblies were the elders, i.e. the full citizens of the community. While it is not entirely certain how such citizenship was defined, it is not unlikely that possession of house and property was an important factor. If this was the case, then it is clear that the local assembly would not always have been representative, for the property-owning qualification which applied may have excluded a number of citizens from participating therein. Indeed, it was suggested that the plight of the widow in Israel was probably due to the fact that, in general, she would have possessed no land of her own and would consequently have been deprived of any representation in the local assembly. In fact, the oracles of Isaiah make it clear that the widow and orphan suffered on two accounts. On the one hand, they were being deprived of the justice due to them in the lawcourt (Is. 1:17, 23), and on the other hand, decrees were being issued which had the effect of depriving them of any property upon which they might have some claim (Is. 10:1-4). We have been concerned to show that these two factors were interrelated, for one's position in the community and one's right to representation in the assembly were contingent upon possession of property.

The provision of levirate marriage was clearly designed to remedy both of these deficiencies, at least so far as the childless widow was concerned. On the one hand, it would have allowed the widow to gain some benefit from her husband's estate by providing her with a son who could inherit the property; on the other hand, marriage to the levir would have afforded her with some measure of protection and support, since he, in his capacity as a land-owning citizen, would have been entitled to represent the widow in the legal assembly. However, this provision would have been somewhat limited in its effect, and there may have been many cases of widowhood in Israel where the levirate simply did not occur.

The above considerations suggest that the accusations of Isaiah concerning the administration of justice in the legal assembly were not necessarily based on specific stipulations found in the law, for these would not always have been an effective means to remedy the situation with which the prophet was confronted. Moreover, it is doubtful whether Isaiah's concern with justice reflects a similar concern expressed in the wisdom literature, for the sayings of the wise can often be shown to be diametrically opposed to the teaching of the prophet. Similarly, the evidence is too vague and general to support the view that Isaiah's words were here based on the utterances of his contemporary, Amos.

Chapter Five
CONCLUSION

In the foregoing discussion we have examined in some detail the role of tradition in the teaching of the prophet Isaiah. Our investigation has shown that a number of attempts have been made to trace the source of Isaiah's ethical pronouncements and that different conclusions have been reached by various scholars concerning the origin of the prophet's teaching. Some believe that Isaiah was primarily dependent upon, and influenced by, the legal tradition, while others stress his use of wisdom vocabulary, and still others have emphasised his dependence upon the prophetic tradition itself. In the present study, however, we have been concerned to show that the whole question of the influence of tradition on the thought of Isaiah is one which is fraught with problems, and our purpose has been to draw attention to some of the difficulties which arise when the teaching of the prophet is viewed against a traditionary background. Some attempt must now be made to summarise our general conclusions and to draw out some implications which arise from the present investigation.

Our first major conclusion concerns the influence of the Sinaitic covenant upon the thought and vocabulary of Isaiah. It was argued that much of the evidence cited in favour of a treaty or covenantal background of Is. 1:2-3 readily admits of other and more satisfactory explanations. It was suggested, for example, that such notions as Israel's rebellion (pāšaᶜ) against Yahweh or Israel's claim to "know" (yādaᶜ) God are perfectly intelligible in the context of Israel's own religious life and experience, and that it was neither necessary nor judicious to turn to the treaty or the covenant for an explanation of these terms. Moreover, it was argued that the use of the "father-son" analogy need not be taken to indicate a "suzerain-vassal" relationship, since the metaphor may have been used by Isaiah simply to suggest that the relationship between Yahweh and Israel was not something which was based on purely legal or contractual grounds.

But the fact that we cannot reconstruct a covenant ideology derived from the ancient Near Eastern vassal-treaties and make this a fundamental presupposition of the prophet's teaching need not be taken to indicate that Isaiah had no knowledge at all of a covenant between Yahweh and Israel or that such a covenant was a late innovation which was only introduced by the Deuteronomists in the seventh century B.C. The early provenance of the covenant in Israel may still be maintained even though serious doubts must be raised concerning the connection of this covenant with the vassal-treaties of the ancient Near East.

However, it is unlikely that the ethical concern of Isaiah was conditioned by this covenant relationship to the extent to which some scholars have suggested. It may be that the prophet saw certain weaknesses in the idea of a "covenant", and regarded the concept as inadequate to convey the precise nature of the relationship which existed between Yahweh and his people /l/. The notion of a "covenant" may have been construed by the people in an external, legalistic way, and it may have engendered in them a smug confidence and a belief that Yahweh was irrevocably committed to defend Israel even when the people had neglected the covenant demands. Since the covenant had come to be regarded in this way, the prophets deliberately avoided not only the term berît but also the very notion for which that word was a symbol. This, as was suggested, may account for the use made by the prophets of other categories to describe the relation between Yahweh and Israel, for by using such analogies as that of the "father and son" or "husband and wife", the prophets were able to lift this relationship out of the purely contractual sphere, and emphasise that Israel was expected to serve Yahweh from a sense of spontaneous respect and affection rather than out of a sense of duty or obligation.

The relation of the prophets to the concept of the covenant has recently been broached from a somewhat different angle, since some scholars have argued that the prophets relied upon a tradition of covenant curses in announcing the judgement which awaited Israel. In the treaties of the ancient Near East, solemn curses were invoked upon those who violated the provisions imposed by the suzerain, and it has been suggested that the curses announced by the prophets were seen by them to be the inevitable consequence that would attend Israel's neglect of the covenant obligations demanded by Yahweh. F.C. Fensham and D.R. Hillers, in particular, have noted many parallels between the curses contained in the treaties and those found in the prophetic threats of judgement, and they have concluded that a

114

strong correlation exists between the two types of malediction
/2/. Such a correlation, it is argued, provides a further indication that the prophetic indictments were formulated in terms
of covenant violation, for the impending judgement which they
announced was an expression of malediction which followed the
breaking of the covenant-relationship.

However, such conclusions must be viewed with some
caution. In the first place, it is clearly mistaken to assume that
the only possible source of blessing or curse was the covenant-
or treaty-form, for the fact is that both the curse and blessing
are found in many sources throughout the ancient Near East
and are by no means limited to treaties /3/. Thus the fact that
the prophetic oracles on the one hand and the Aramaic and
Assyrian treaties on the other share a common stock of imagery
hardly necessitates the presupposition of a common source or a
direct cultural borrowing. In this regard, Hillers admits that
what he has termed "treaty-curses" are for the most part
simply traditional maledictions which happen to occur in
treaties /4/. Nevertheless, he insists that the similarity between specific calamities announced by the prophets and the
curses invoked for treaty-violation among Israel's neighbours is
too strong to avoid the conclusion that the prophets were
indebted to the curse-motif found in the treaties of the ancient
Near East /5/. However, the evidence we possess is insufficient
to support such a conclusion, and it is far more probable that
many of the calamities predicted by the prophets - such as
famine, drought, bloodshed, fire, sword, seizure of fields - were
simply the usual occurrences which might have been expected
when a city or village was attacked by a foreign invader. In
fact, the judgements announced by the prophets may have been
nothing more than projections into the future of the type of
calamities which tended to recur in the ancient world /6/. Thus
the similarity between their pronouncements of doom and the
threats implied in the covenant curses may simply have been
fortuitous, and it certainly cannot be used as an argument to
demonstrate the centrality of the covenant concept in the
thought of the prophets.

Our second conclusion concerns the use made by Isaiah of
ancient Israel's legal tradition, and it was suggested that the
prophet's concern with social justice did not primarily involve
such duties as are laid down in any extant law code. In this
regard, we have endeavoured to raise questions concerning the
limits of legislative competence and the extent to which the

law could usefully be employed to tackle the social problems with which the prophet had to contend. We have seen that there is often ground for scepticism regarding the effectiveness of the law to combat social abuses and to correct injustice and oppression. A number of reasons have been advanced in support of this conclusion. In the first place, it was observed that not all social control could be achieved through the legal order, and it was suggested that an important part of the prophet's task was to make clear the various aspects of man's social responsibility which could not be controlled through legislation. Further, the powerful citizens of the community may have taken advantage of the ambiguities present in the legal system in order to achieve their own ends. Indeed, the possibility was suggested that many of the injustices against which Isaiah inveighed were perpetrated on perfectly "legal" grounds. It was argued, for example, that some of the methods employed by the wealthy to acquire land at the expense of the smallholders were not technically illegal, for property could easily have been appropriated through foreclosure of mortgage or through debt-bondage, i.e. through procedures which were permitted by the law. These, of course, were just some of the ways by which the wealthy might have taken advantage of the various loopholes present in the legal system. Other methods of circumventing the law may also have been utilised by them, and it is precisely for this reason that the law would only have had a limited effect in preventing social abuses. This, in turn, might explain the paucity of references to specific legal provisions in the oracles of the eighth-century prophets, for if the law was indeed ineffective in combating the abuses in the social system, then appeal to particular stipulations would have added but little weight to the prophet's indictments. Instead of a direct appeal to the law, therefore, the prophets were content to emphasise that people should treat each other with a mutual respect and affection which transcended legal duty.

The third tradition which has been thought to lie behind Isaiah's teaching is that of wisdom. The influence of wisdom on the prophets has been argued by scholars partly on the basis of a similarity in form, style and vocabulary between the wisdom literature and the eighth-century prophetic utterances. However, this approach has rightly been criticised on the ground that many of the literary devices employed by the prophets - such as the numerical saying or the rhetorical questions - are too common to be regarded as indicative of one particular

116

tradition. The other argument that has been advanced in favour of a wisdom background is the fact that certain sapiential themes and motifs reappear in the oracles of the prophets, and that the teaching of the prophets on various issues reflects in many ways that of the wisdom writers. However, too much weight should not be attached to this argument, for the wisdom writers merely articulate the moral standards and beliefs of the community at large, and the fact that the prophets occasionally shared some of these standards and beliefs is hardly surprising and need not be taken to indicate the influence of wisdom on their own thoughts and ideas. In fact, there can be no doubt that the sage often does share the same interests as the prophet: they both agree on the importance of social justice (Prov. 17:15; cf. Am. 2:6) especially in the economic order (Prov. 11:1; 16:11; cf. Am. 8:4-6), and both are concerned to defend rights in property (Prov. 24:15; cf. Is. 5:8-10) and to condemn bribery and corruption (Prov. 15:27; 18:5; cf. Is. 5:23). The difficulty, however, is to establish adequate controls for showing what degree of similarity in such matters of form and content between wisdom and prophecy is necessary before one can confidently claim the influence of one tradition upon the other. This difficulty is exacerbated by the fact that certain themes which recur in both traditions - such as respect for the needy and oppressed - are common to many other traditions also, so that the prophets cannot always be shown to have any specific provision of wisdom in mind. The problem is further complicated by the fact that the possibility must remain open that it was the sages who imitated the prophetic manner of speech /7/; thus even if certain similarities do exist between prophecy and wisdom, and even if these similarities were of such a nature as to suggest a direct borrowing, it need not necessarily be concluded that the prophets were influenced by the wisdom tradition, since the reverse might also be true.

Further, it should not be left unremarked that the book of Proverbs contains wisdom material which is very divergent in form, viewpoint and content, and scholars who posit the influence of wisdom on the prophets have tended to overlook the fact that some fundamental differences exist between the two traditions in their approach to life and in their characteristic ways of thought. Thus although bribery, for example, is roundly condemned by the prophets and in certain passages in the wisdom literature, other passages in the book of Proverbs could be cited which would be diametrically opposed to everything the prophets had to say on the subject of the corruption prevalent in the legal procedure. Naturally, the fact that there exists within the wisdom literature itself such opposing philosophies and divergent ideas on various issues makes the task of determining the extent of wisdom influence particularly difficult, since it becomes almost impossible to identify in any precise way what the "normative" teaching of wisdom was on any specific subject.

It must be concluded, as a result of our investigation, that prophecy and wisdom are to be regarded as parallel forms of spiritual and literary activity, and that the prophet and sage each expressed his concern from his own particular vantage point. Prophecy and wisdom, therefore, played each its own distinctive part in the cultural and spiritual life of Israel, and no question of the dependence of one tradition upon the other need arise.

The final conclusion to which the present investigation points is that the arguments which have been advanced in support of Isaiah's dependence upon the oracles of his contemporary, Amos, are quite unconvincing, since any similarity which may exist between them can be adequately explained as due to the similar circumstances in which both prophets were placed and the similar problems with which they had to contend. The general social conditions were much the same in Israel as in Judah during this period, and any points of contact between the two prophets may simply be due to the fact that their picture of social conditions largely coincide. The linguistic affinities between Amos and Isaiah are not so striking as to warrant the assumption of a direct dependence of one prophet upon the other, and the argument that the differences are due to Isaiah's attempts to go beyond his Vorlage simply cannot be sustained. It must be concluded, therefore, that Isaiah's indictments were the product of his own experience of the evils prevalent in Judah, and it is quite unnecessary to assume that his thoughts were the product of a theoretical reflection upon the doctrines of his contemporary.

It is clear from the present investigation that the general tendency of scholars who have examined the origin of Isaiah's ethical teaching has been to broach the subject by inquiring into the nature of the traditions which could have been accessible to the prophet and which may have served as a model for his own utterances. This procedure, however, is methodologically un-satisfactory, for it anticipates conclusions that should arise

118

V Conclusion

from an examination of the text itself, and it is often the case
that the preconceptions of commentators have prevented them
from approaching the subject with the necessary detachment.
Consequently, the present investigation has been based on a
detailed exegesis of some passages in Isaiah where social and
ethical problems predominate, and it was concluded that it is
difficult to identify with any certainty the source of the
prophet's moral instruction. Indeed, we have seen that it is
doubtful if we can speak of Isaiah's "dependence" on any one
tradition, for it is probable that the prophet borrowed -
consciously or unconsciously - from the total culture in which
he lived. Thus, to speak of the "intellectual home" of a prophet
in this context is misleading, for the position of the prophet was
more broadly-based than modern critical analysis might
suggest. While Isaiah does exhort and admonish his hearers, this
is almost always done in ad hoc fashion in relation to the
specific situations with which he was confronted. Since the
wisdom teacher, the law-giver and the prophets were often concerned with similar situations, it is hardly surprising that their
vistas of thought and modes of expression should sometimes
overlap. Moreover, these traditions were all grounded in a
common faith and each recognised that the qualities which
Yahweh demanded of men included a sense of compassion
combined with humility, honesty and integrity. These were the
virtues in which Yahweh took delight, and this was the teaching
of the law and the prophets upon which our Lord himself set his
seal (Mt. 22:37ff.).

1   Hempel, Das Ethos des Alten Testaments; van Oyen, Ethik des Alten Testaments.

Notes to Chapter One, Part I
PROPHECY AND TRADITION

1   Wellhausen, Prolegomena, pp.392ff.
2   Ibid., pp.417ff.
3   Ibid., pp.399ff.
4   The following comment by Wellhausen with regard to the significance of the prophets is particularly illuminating: "They do not preach on set texts; they speak out of the spirit which judges all things and itself is judged of no man. Where do they ever lean on any other authority than the truth of what they say; where do they rest on any other foundation than their own certainty?... While acting in the most creative way they feel entirely passive: the homo tantum et audacia which may with perfect justice be applied to such men as Elijah, Amos, and Isaiah, is with them equivalent to deus tantum et servitus. But their creed is not to be found in any book. It is barbarism, in dealing with such a phenomenon, to distort its physiognomy by introducing the law" (ibid., pp.398f.).
5   Cf. Duhm, Die Theologie, pp.168ff.
6   Ibid., pp.77ff. Significantly, Duhm argued that the word nābî' should not generally be translated as "prophet", for the term should be reserved to designate the man who uttered while in an ecstatic state and in the possession of a higher power. Cf. Duhm, Israels Propheten (second edition, 1922), p.81.
7   Weber, Das antike Judentum.
8   Causse, Du Groupe ethnique, pp.61ff.; see also his article, "Les Prophètes", pp.97-140. For a discussion of Causse's contribution to the sociological approach to Old Testament studies, see Kimbrough, "Une Conception sociologique", pp. 313-26; idem, Israelite Religion, passim.
9   Hölscher, Die Profeten, pp.189ff. For a more recent discussion of the psychology of prophetic inspiration, see

120

Lindblom, Prophecy, pp.197ff., 299ff.

10   Robinson, Prophecy, pp.39ff.

11   Ibid., pp.45f. Duhm himself later came to place greater emphasis on the emotional and ecstatic experiences of the prophets. Cf. Israels Propheten, pp.95f.

12   Heschel, The Prophets, pp.221ff., 351ff.

13   Alt, Die Ursprunge des israelitischen Rechts.

14   Cf. Gerstenberger, Wesen und Herkunft, pp.110ff., who argued that the origin of the apodictic form should rather be traced to the instruction imparted by the father or tribal chief to the younger members of the clan. See, further, his article, "Covenant and Commandment", pp.45-51. Cf., however, the criticisms of Gerstenberger's position noted by Bright, "The Apodictic Prohibition", pp.200-04.

15   Cf. Meek, Hebrew Origins (revised edition, 1950), pp.72f.; MacKenzie, "The Formal Aspect", pp.39-44; Rapaport, "The Origins", pp.166f.

16   Gevirtz, "West-Semitic Curses and the Problem of the Origins of Hebrew Law", pp.137-58, finds the apodictic-style form in west Semitic curses which served as prohibitions threatening divine punishment.

17   Cf. Mendenhall, "Ancient Oriental and Biblical Law", pp.29f.

18   Würthwein, "Amos-Studien", pp.40ff., argued that Amos' indictments were firmly based in Israel's legal tradition. In a similar vein, Bach, "Gottesrecht und weltliches Recht in der Verkündigung des Propheten Amos", Festschrift Günther Dehn, pp.23-34, sought to demonstrate that Amos based his accusations solely on the apodictic law.

19   Wellhausen, Prolegomena, pp.417-19.

20   Mendenhall, "Covenant Forms in Israelite Tradition", pp.50-76. Mendenhall's observations have been developed by Baltzer, The Covenant Formulary, and Beyerlin, Origins and History of the Oldest Sinaitic Traditions.

21   Mendenhall, "Covenant Forms", pp.65-7

22   Cf. Beyerlin, Origins and History, pp.145ff.

23   Cf., e.g., Bright, A History of Israel (revised edition, 1972), pp.146-9; von Rad, Old Testament Theology, i, pp.132f.; Hillers, Covenant: The History of a Biblical Idea, pp.46ff.; Eichrodt, "Covenant and Law", pp.306ff.

24   Eichrodt, for example, had previously argued in favour of an early dating for the covenant concept in Israel in his Theologie des Alten Testaments, i, pp.26ff.

25   Cf. Mendenhall, "Ancient Oriental and Biblical Law", p.42, who claimed that the words of the prophets were "essentially indictments of Israel for breach of covenant". Cf. also Hillers, Covenant, pp.120ff.; Moriarty, "Prophet and Covenant", pp.817-33.

26   Cf. Clements, Prophecy and Covenant,'pp.45ff.

27   See below, pp.42ff.

28   Cf. Porteous, "The Basis of the Ethical Teaching of the Prophets", pp.143ff.

29   Eng. tr., Old Testament Theology, ii, Edinburgh, 1965.

30   Ibid., pp.176ff.

31   Perlitt, Bundestheologie im Alten Testament, WMANT 36, 1969.

32   Ibid., pp.129ff.

33   Nicholson, Exodus and Sinai in History and Tradition, pp.76f.; C.F. Whitley, The Prophetic Achievement, pp.24ff.

34   McCarthy, Treaty and Covenant, pp.152ff.

35   Ibid., pp.158f. Beyerlin's objection (Origins and History, pp.53f.) that the possibility of curse or blessing lay dormant in the Decalogue according to whether the stipulations were obeyed or neglected is rightly criticised by McCarthy on the ground that the Hittite suzerainty-treaties contained the curse-blessing formula as an independent feature of the treaty and not as something merely implicit in the stipulations of the overlord.

36   McCarthy, Treaty and Covenant, pp.109ff.

37   Cf. Clements, Prophecy and Tradition, pp.41ff., which represents a modification of some of his earlier views.

38   Fohrer, "Tradition und Interpretation im Alten Testament", pp.24ff.; idem, "Remarks on Modern Interpretation of the Prophets", pp.309-19.

39   Ibid., p.316.

40   Vollmer, Geschichtliche Rückblicke und Motive in der Prophetie des Amos, Hosea und Jesaja, BZAW 119, 1971.

41   Cf., e.g., Clements, Prophecy and Covenant, p.55, who commented: "We may confidently claim...that when the pre-exilic prophets referred to the events of the exodus, and of Israel's desert origin, they were referring to the fact that Israel was a covenant people, and were appealing to the fact of the divine grace which had originated that covenant. The prophetic appeal to the election of Israel was an appeal to the covenant".

42   Vollmer, Geschichtliche Rückblicke, pp.29-33.

43   Ibid., p.209.

44 Melugin, "The Conventional and the Creative in Isaiah's Judgment Oracles", pp.301-11. See further, by the same author, "The Typical versus the Unique among the Hebrew Prophets", pp.331-41.

Part II

1 von Rad, Old Testament Theology, i, pp.190ff.
2 von Rad, Old Testament Theology, ii, p.137, comments with regard to Amos: "At all events, it is a quality of heart and mind that he finds lacking in the upper classes; the breach of particular commandments is certainly not in question, for there was no commandment which forbade reclining on ornate beds or anointing oneself with choicest oil, no more than there was any which obliged people to be grieved at the damage done to Joseph. What Amos refers to, therefore, is a general attitude, the way men should live together, and jointly and severally be fellow sufferers in the experiences of God's people".
3 Ibid., pp.186f.
4 Daube, "Direct and Indirect Causation in Biblical Law", pp.257-61, suggests that the absence of legislation concerning many offences which might be expected to have been regulated by the law was due to the fact that it was only those laws which were in need of reform or those cases which presented certain difficulties or ambiguities that engaged the attention of the legislator; the most usual or ordinary cases were therefore not taken into account.
5 Cf. Snaith, "The Daughters of Zelophehad", pp.124-7; Weingreen, "The Case of the Daughters of Zelophchad", pp.518-22.
6 Cf. Weingreen, "The Case of the Woodgatherer (Numbers XV 32-36)", pp.361-4; Phillips, "The Case of the Woodgatherer Reconsidered", pp.125-8.
7 See below, pp.66ff.
8 See below, pp.100-102.
9 Phillips, "The Interpretation of 2 Samuel xii 5-6", pp.242-4, suggests that David's reply to Nathan to the effect that the rich citizen who stole the poor man's ewe lamb deserved to die, reflects the inadequacy of the laws governing theft, for the damages prescribed in such a case (fourfold restitution) may have proved little deterrent to the rich who could have afforded to take the risk of being caught.
10 Cf. Duhm, Die Theologie der Propheten, pp.244f.
11 For a discussion of this development, see Clements, A

Century of Old Testament Study, pp.99ff.

12   Cf. Albright, "Some Canaanite-Phoenician Sources of Hebrew Wisdom", pp.1-15.

13   The Solomonic origin of wisdom in Israel has been discussed by Alt, "Die Weisheit Salomos", cols.139-44 (= KS, ii, pp.90-9); Whybray, Wisdom in Proverbs, pp.20f. Scott, "Solomon and the Beginnings of Wisdom in Israel", pp.262-79, argued that the narratives linking Solomon with the origins of literary wisdom in Israel were post-exilic in date and legendary in character, and he suggested that the wisdom movement first became influential at the time of Isaiah and Hezekiah. Later, however, Scott modified his view and claimed that although the accounts concerning Solomon's connection with wisdom had been embellished by certain legendary accretions, there was "undoubtedly some substance to the tradition that associated with his name the flourishing of the early Wisdom movement" (Proverbs. Ecclesiastes, p.xxxiii; cf. also, The Way of Wisdom, pp.13-15, 95).

14   For a recent discussion, see Olivier, "Schools and Wisdom Literature", pp.49-60.

15   Fichtner, "Jesaja unter den Weisen", cols.75-80.

16   Ibid., cols.79f.; cf. Anderson, "Was Isaiah a Scribe?", pp.57f., who suggests that Isaiah was originally a scribe who served as counsellor to the king. This, he argues, would explain his ready access to the monarch and also his concern with the international situation which would have been precipitated through his involvement with the diplomatic documents kept in the royal court.

17   Fichtner, "Jesaja unter den Weisen", cols.79f.; cf. Martin-Achard, "Sagesse de Dieu et sagesse humaine chez Esaïe", pp.137-44.

18   Cf. Lindblom, "Wisdom in the Old Testament Prophets", pp.192-204.

19   Whedbee, Isaiah and Wisdom, Nashville - New York, 1971.

20   Fichtner, however, had argued that all traces of wisdom-forms in the other eighth-century prophets were to be regarded as later additions ("Jesaja unter den Weisen", cols.75f.).

21   Cf. Terrien, "Amos and Wisdom", pp.108-15.

22   Wolff, Amos the Prophet. The Man and his Background, Eng. tr., Philadelphia, 1973; cf. also his commentary, Joel and Amos, Eng. tr., Philadelphia, 1977.

23   Cf. Crenshaw, "The Influence of the Wise upon Amos.

The 'Doxologies of Amos' and Job 5:9-16; 9:5-10", pp.42-52; Schmid, "Amos. Zur Frage nach der 'geistigen Heimat' des Propheten", pp.85-103.

24   Cf. Whybray, The Intellectual Tradition in the Old Testament, pp.71f.

25   Cf. Clements, Prophecy and Tradition, pp.81f.

26   Cf., e.g., Scott, The Way of Wisdom, pp.121f.

27   Cf. Clements, Prophecy and Tradition, p.78, n.9.

28   Whedbee, Isaiah and Wisdom, p.24.

29   Ibid., pp. 151f.

30   Ibid., pp. 130ff.

31   Ibid., pp.61ff.; cf. Blanchette, "The Wisdom of God in Isaia", pp.413-23.

32   Whedbee, Isaiah and Wisdom, pp.114ff. But cf. von Rad, Old Testament Theology, ii, p.162, who argues that the concept of Yahweh's "plan" (Cēṣāh) was the prophet's own innovation.

33   Whedbee, Isaiah and Wisdom, pp.143ff. Cf. Cazelles, "Les Débuts de la sagesse en Israël", p.32, who appropriately comments with regard to Is. 28:23ff.: "C'est un des nombreux cas où le Prophète utilise le langage des sages pour mieux les combattre".

34   McKane, Prophets and Wise Men, SBT 44, 1965.

35   Ibid., pp.23ff.

36   As McKane (ibid., p.48) observes, this did not mean that they were indifferent to matters of religious or ethical import, but simply that such considerations could play no part in their political decisions: "That this wisdom does not admit piety is to be accounted for by the fact that it is a wisdom of statecraft, that its practitioners have to take the world as they find it and that in their approach to its complex reality they do not permit themselves the luxury of religious or ethical assumptions".

37   Ibid., pp.48ff. Cf. Gunkel, "Vergeltung", col. 1532, who similarly held the view that Hebrew Wisdom was originally secular in character and that the religious motive was only introduced at a later stage.

38   von Rad, Old Testament Theology, i, pp.441ff.; cf. further, his remarks in Wisdom in Israel, pp.62ff.

39   Whybray, The Intellectual Tradition in the Old Testament, pp.15ff.

40   Ibid., pp.17f.

41   Ibid., p.31.

42.   Whybray himself had previously argued that in such passages as Jer. 18:18 the term ḥākām was apparently used in a

technical sense "to designate a specific class of men who, together with the priests and the prophets, constituted the basis of established society at that time" (Wisdom in Proverbs, p.18).

43   Cf. Clements, Prophecy and Tradition, pp.82f.

44   Fey, Amos und Jesaja, WMANT 12, 1963. Some earlier scholars had suggested the possibility that Isaiah may have been influenced by the teaching of Amos. Cf. Gray, Isaiah I-XXVII, p.lxxxv.

45   Cf., e.g., Zimmerli, The Law and the Prophets, pp.73f.; Fohrer, Introduction to the Old Testament, p.372.

46   Fohrer, Introduction, pp.40f., 359f.

47   For what follows, see Fey, Amos und Jesaja, pp.9ff.

48   The "woe-form" is discussed below, pp.83-6.

Notes to Chapter Two
ISRAEL'S REBELLION AGAINST YAHWEH (Is. 1:2-3)

1   Cf. Wildberger, Jesaja, p.8; Eissfeldt, Introduction, p.309.

2   Fohrer, "Jesaja 1", p.253; cf. Whitehouse, Isaiah I - XXXIX, p.89, who claimed that this opening chapter "may be regarded as a characteristic summary of all that is most essential in Isaiah's teaching".

3   Cf. Eichrodt, Der Heilige, p.25; Kaiser, Isaiah 1-12, pp.6f.

4   This view is discussed below, pp.51ff.

5   Cf. Robinson, "Higher Criticism", p.200.

6   The possibility of a direct dependence on the oracles of Amos does not arise in this particular instance.

7   Cf., e.g., Whedbee, Isaiah and Wisdom, pp.26ff.

8   Cf., e.g., Wildberger, Jesaja, pp.8-17.

9   Mendenhall, "Covenant Forms", pp.50-76.

10   Ibid., pp.58-60.

11   Ibid., p.54.

12   Ibid., pp.61ff. Mendenhall developed this view by suggesting that the Decalogue of Ex. 20 was to be regarded as part of a treaty-like covenant between Yahweh and Israel. This possibility was further explored by Beyerlin, Origins and History, pp.49ff., and by Baltzer, The Covenant Formulary, pp.19ff.

13   McCarthy, Treaty and Covenant, pp.39f., claims that this was one of the most stable features of the Hittite treaties, for the list of gods was practically never omitted from these

documents.

14   Cf. Wiseman, "The Vassal-Treaties", p.22.

15   Cf. Dupont-Sommer, Les Inscriptions, p.19.

16   ANET, p.205.

17   Cf. Langdon and Gardiner, "The Treaty of Alliance", p.194.

18   Mendenhall, "Covenant Forms", p.66.

19   Ibid., pp.60, 66.

20   Cf., e.g., Wildberger, Jesaja, pp.9ff.

21   Cf. Delcor, "Les attaches littéraires", p.20, who argues that it is in "un contexte d'Alliance qu'apparaît l'évocation des éléments de la nature".

22   Huffmon, "The Covenant Lawsuit", p.293.

23   Cf. Harvey, Le Plaidoyer prophétique, pp.86f.

24   Cf., for example, the following extract from a Hittite prayer: "Gods and goddesses of king and queen, ye who have been invoked (and) ye who have not been invoked; ye in whose temples king and queen worship officiating as priests, (and) ye in whose temples. they do not! Gods (and) goddesses...dark nether world, heaven (and) earth, clouds (and) winds, thunder (and) lightning, place of assembly where the gods meet in assembly!" (ANET, p.398).

25   Cf., for example, the following words which occur in praise of Ishtar: "At the thought of thy name heaven and earth tremble/The Gods tremble; the Anunnaki stand in awe" (ANET, p.384).

26   See below, pp.54f.

27   Fohrer, Jesaja, i, pp.24f.

28   Cf. Huffmon, "The Covenant Lawsuit", p.294, who describes Is. 1:2b as a historical prologue which is presented in terms of a family history.

29   Cf. Thompson, "The Near Eastern Suzerain-Vassal Concept", pp.6ff.

30   Cf. McCarthy, Old Testament Covenant, p.33, who notes that covenants and treaties were often thought of as establishing "a kind of quasi-familial unity".

31   Cf. Fensham, "Father and Son", pp.121-35. It is possible, however, that the terms "father-son" in the treaties did not always designate a "suzerain-vassal" relationship. G. Dossin, for example, has expressed the view that the terms "father" and "son" were sometimes employed simply as a mark of deference and respect, and carried no connotations of political subordination (see ARM, v, p.124). Dossin cites two examples in

support of his view. The first concerns Aplaḫanda, king of Carchemish who, writing to Iasmaḫ-Addu, designates himself in the introductory formula as "the brother" (a-ḫu-ka) of Iasmaḫ-Addu. It seems, then, that Aplaḫanda regarded himself as a "brother" (and therefore an equal) of Iasmaḫ-Addu, and yet in line 17 (of a broken text) he refers to Šamši-Addu, Iasmaḫ-Addu's father, as "my father", presumably out of respect for the older king. The second example concerns Iatâr-Ami (Aplaḫanda's son) who writes as a "son" to Zimri-Lim, the king of Mari. Here, again, the term may be no more than a mark of respect, since Zimri-Lim spoke of Aplaḫanda as his "brother" suggesting that the parties were, in fact, on equal terms. Dossin's view, however, has been criticised by Munn-Rankin, "Diplomacy in Western Asia", pp.81-3, who argues that in these particular cases the terms "father" and "son" were used to designate the relationship between a vassal and his overlord, since Carchemish certainly acknowledged Assyrian suzerainty, and Iatâr-Ami was probably a vassal of Zimri-Lim. She does concede, however, that in general the terms "brotherhood" and "sonship" are "not reliable guides to political status" (p.84).

32   McCarthy, "Notes on the Love of God", pp.144-7.

33   Ibid., p.147.

34   Cf. McKenzie, "The Divine Sonship of Men", p.326; idem, "The Divine Sonship of Israel", pp.320-31. Daube, "Rechts-gedanken", pp.35-7, on the basis of the designation of Israel as Yahweh's son considers the entire exodus narrative from the standpoint of the paternal right of redemption. Cf. also Sklba, "The Redeemer", pp.13-17.

35   Cf. Kaiser, Isaiah 1-12, pp.7f. As a divine epithet, ʼab is applied to El, and in some texts he is called ʼab ʼadm, "father of mankind". See Herdner, Corpus des tablettes, ii, 14 [IK] I, 37, 43 etc. Such pagan notions may explain the paucity of references to Yahweh as "father" in the Old Testament, for such a notion may have been misunderstood to imply the existence of a physical, natural blood-relationship between Yahweh and his people.

36   As Vollmer, Geschichtliche Rückblicke, p.147, observes, the precise occasion when Yahweh adopted Israel as a "son" is not mentioned, nor does the prophet specify the occasion when Israel is supposed to have rebelled against her God.

37   Cf. Eissfeldt, Das Lied Moses, pp.15-25, who reviews the dates assigned to the poem, and argues that the composition of

the song should be ascribed to the middle of the eleventh century B.C. His arguments were accepted by Albright, "Some Remarks", pp.339-46, who had previously dated the song in a later period. An early date has also been suggested by Cassuto, "The Song of Moses", pp.41-6, and Skehan, "The Structure of the Song of Moses", pp.153-63. There are other scholars, however, who tend to favour a later date. Cf., e.g., Driver, Deuteronomy, pp.345-7.

38   Cf. Wright, "The Terminology", p.410. Bright, A History (revised edition, 1972), p.98, notes that such names are rare after the tenth century B.C., but were quite common until then. For a discussion of the personal names with "father" or "brother" as a theophoric element, see Noth, Die israelitischen Personennamen, pp.66-75.

39   For an example of this usage of the term in the vassal-treaties of Esarhaddon, see Wiseman, "Vassal-Treaties", pp.34, 52, etc.

40   Cf., e.g., von Rad, Old Testament Theology, i, p.263. For the use of the term in a political context, see Knierim, Die Hauptbegriffe, pp.150f.

41   Cf., e.g., Limburg, The Lawsuit of God, pp.257-64.

42   Cf. Knierim, Die Hauptbegriffe, pp.178f., who emphasises that the root pšᶜ can be used of many different kinds of offences, and can occur in very diverse Sitze im Leben.

43   Huffmon, "The Treaty Background", pp.31-7; cf. also Huffmon and Parker, "A Further Note", pp.36-8, where additional evidence from an Akkadian text from Mari and a Ugaritic text from Ras Shamra is cited to support the proposed semantic connection.

44   Cf. Bergren, The Prophets and the Law, pp.118f.; Limburg, The Lawsuit of God, pp.266-9. Cf. also his article, "The Root ריב', p.303.

45   Cf. von Loewenclau, "Zur Auslegung", p.307.

46   Hoffmann, Die Intention, pp.84f., suggests that the prophet's accusation here gains in meaning once it is realised that among Isaiah's hearers were those who boasted in their own cleverness and insight (cf. Is. 5:21).

47   Cf., e.g., Huffmon, "The Covenant Lawsuit", p.286.

48   Cf. McCarthy, "Covenant in the Old Testament", p.239, who suggests that the presence of the lawsuit in the prophetic literature indicates that the prophets knew something like the treaty-form, and applied it to the relationship between Yahweh and Israel. The study of J. Harvey on the covenant lawsuit must

be mentioned here, for he has argued that the origin of this form is to be found in the letters of accusation which a suzerain delivered to a rebellious vassal who had broken the stipulations of the treaty which united them. Harvey concludes that in the prophetic lawsuits, Yahweh is represented as the suzerain who charges the prophet to address his erring vassals and accuse them of violating the covenant that had bound them together. Thus Harvey seeks the origin of the covenant lawsuit "dans le droit international, et plus précisément dans le même droit international qui a fourni le schéma de l'alliance" ("Le 'rîb-pattern'", p.180; see also his modified position in Le Plaidoyer prophétique). The study of Limburg, "The Root ריב", pp.291-304, seems to point in the same direction, for he argues that the word rîb belonged essentially to the sphere of international relations, especially international treaties. The arguments adduced by Harvey, however, are open to criticism on the following grounds: 1. There is a considerable lapse of time between the diplomatic documents of the second millennium B.C. cited by Harvey and the speeches of the prophets in the eighth and seventh centuries B.C. 2. The documents which Harvey cites represent indictments of individual rulers whereas the prophetic lawsuits are a general condemnation of the inhabitants of Israel and Judah. 3. The style in which the complaint is made is not always the same in the two cases, for in the diplomatic documents the suzerain addresses the vassal directly (as, for example, in the letter of Iarîm-Lim, king of Aleppo, to Iasub-Iaḫad, king of Dir), but in some of the passages which Harvey cites as lawsuits (e.g. Is.1:2-3, 10-20) the accusation is formulated in the third person style. For criticisms of Harvey's approach, see Amsler, "Le Thème du procès", pp.124f.

49   Cf. Harvey, Le Plaidoyer prophétique, p.93, who claims that in the covenant lawsuit "l'accusation d'infidélité est toujours étroitement liée à l'alliance et plus précisément, dans la grande majorité des cas, à la formule de l'alliance sinaïtique". See also Nielsen, Yahweh as Prosecutor, pp.27-9.

50   Wright, "The Lawsuit of God", pp.52-4.

51   Cf., e.g., Huffmon, "The Covenant Lawsuit", pp.291-3.

52   See further, below, pp.54f. It must again be emphasised that the invocation of "heaven and earth" is too widespread in biblical and extra-biblical documents for one to be able to limit this feature to a particular genre. In this regard, Huffmon (ibid., p.289) certainly goes too far when he claims that the

address to the natural elements is used "only within the framework of passages that represent, imitate, or resemble the 'lawsuit' ".

53   See below, p.53.

54   See above, pp.46f.

55   Harvey, "Le 'rîb-pattern'", p.178, distinguishes between the lawsuits which end with a sentence (which correspond to the documents containing a declaration of war by a suzerain on an unfaithful vassal), and those which merely end with a "warning" (which correspond to the letters of ultimatum sent by a suzerain to a vassal who had begun to turn aside from the stipulations of the alliance). Harvey, therefore, classifies Is. 1:2-3, 10-20 as a rîb of "warning".

56   Harvey, Le Plaidoyer prophétique, pp.36ff., argues that the essential elements of the lawsuit can be discerned in Is. 1:2-3, 10-20. Gemser, "The Rîb- or Controversy-Pattern", p.130, claims that the whole of the first chapter of Isaiah was composed as the "protocol" of the proceedings of a rîb. See also Marshall, "The Structure of Isaiah 1-12", pp.26-8.

57   Cf., e.g., Fohrer, Jesaja, i, pp.24-7. Boecker, Redeformen, pp.83f., argues that Is. 1:2-3 was formulated as an accusation-speech in which the accuser addressed the court concerning a third party.

58   Cf. Vollmer, Geschichtliche Rückblicke, pp.147f.

59   Cf. Boecker, "Anklagereden", p.400, who argues that the literary form known as the lawsuit (Gerichtsrede) stems from the ordinary judicial procedure "at the gate". A similar view had been advocated by Gunkel, Einleitung in die Psalmen, pp.364f. See also Scott, "The Literary Structure", p.179; Westermann, Basic Forms, pp.199f.; Clements, Prophecy and Tradition, pp.19f. Von Waldow, Der Hintergrund, p.20, argues that as regards form the prophetic rîb is derived from the secular legal process current in ancient Israel, but as regards content it is based on the tradition of Yahweh's covenant with Israel.

60   This assumption is made, for example, by Boecker, Redeformen, p.92.

61   Cf. Wildberger, Jesaja, pp.131-4; Fohrer, Jesaja, i, pp.64f.; Scott, "The Book of Isaiah", p.190; Eichrodt, Der Heilige, p.59. Another passage which is thought to reflect judicial procedure is Is. 5:1-7, but this will be omitted from our discussion since it contains many features which are not usually considered to be basic elements of a lawsuit. The various

categories into which these verses have been classified by
different scholars have been discussed by Willis, "The Genre of
Isaiah 5:1-7", pp.337-62.
62   So Wildberger, loc. cit.; Eichrodt, loc. cit.; but cf.
Fohrer, loc. cit., who takes the unit to consist of vv.12-15.
63   Köhler, Deuterojesaja, pp.110ff.
64   This assumption is made, for example, by de Vaux,
Ancient Israel, p.156.
65   For attempts to reconstruct the judicial procedure in
ancient Israel, see Köhler, "Justice in the Gate", pp.149-75;
McKenzie, "Judicial Procedure", pp.100-04; de Vaux, Ancient
Israel, pp.155-7.
66   Cf., e.g., Bright, "Isaiah - I", p.490.
67   Cf., e.g., Skinner, Isaiah I - XXXIX, p.28.
68   Boecker, Redeformen, pp.87-9, has sought to show that
one and the same person could function as both plaintiff and
judge by referring to the account contained in 1 Sam. 22:6ff.,
where Saul is described as sitting under a tamarisk tree with his
spear in his hand and accusing his servants (v.8) and Ahimelech
(v.13) of conspiring against him. Later in the same narrative, he
appears as a "judge" who pronounces the death sentence (v.16).
However, it would be hazardous to draw any far-reaching
conclusions on the basis of this narrative, since it can hardly be
regarded as a straight-forward instance of the operation of the
judicial process. For a further discussion of Saul's judicial role,
see Macholz, "Die Stellung des Königs", pp.160-2.
69   Cf. Wildberger, Jesaja, pp.9f.
70   Cf. Scott, "The Book of Isaiah", p.166.
71   Cf. Bentzen, Introduction, i, pp.199f.; Gunkel, Einleitung
in die Psalmen, p.365.
72   Köhler, Deuterojesaja, p.112.
73   Cf. McCarthy, Treaty and Covenant, pp.109ff.
74   McCarthy (ibid., p.134) notes that the appeal to heaven
and earth as witnesses is a phenomenon which is without
parallel except in the treaty tradition.
75   See above, pp.42ff.
76   Cf. Skinner, Isaiah I - XXXIX, p.3; Driver, Deuteronomy,
p.349.
77   Cf. Tucker, "Witnesses", p.43. Liebesny, "Evidence in
Nuzi", p.132, notes that in Nuzi, also, witnesses were produced
by the litigant himself either of his own accord or upon the
request of the court.
78   Cf., e.g., Eichrodt, Der Heilige, p.59.

79   Wildberger, _Jesaja_, p.16.
80   See below, pp.59-61.
81   Cf., e.g., Eichrodt, _loc. cit._; see also Nielsen, "Das Bild des Gerichts", pp.316f.
82   It may be inquired, for example, whether the accusation implies that the leaders were guilty of corruption and of drawing extortionate interest rates from the poor as Eichrodt (_ibid._) suggests, or whether the prophet here has in mind such offences as robbery, murder and land-grabbing as Fohrer (_Jesaja_, i, p.65) contends.
83   Boecker, "Anklagereden", pp.400-402.
84   Boecker, _Redeformen_, pp.83f.
85   Cf. von Loewenclau, "Zur Auslegung", pp.297f.
86   Cf. Würthwein, "Der Ursprung", p.7.
87   For a discussion of the heavenly council, see Wheeler Robinson, "The Council", pp.151-7.
88   Wright, _The Old Testament_, p.36. Cross, "The Council", p.274, n.3, suggests that the prophetic lawsuits in general should be interpreted in this way, although he concedes that the imagery of the heavenly council has often receded into the background.
89   Huffmon, "The Covenant Lawsuit", pp.290f.
90   Wright, _The Old Testament_, p.36; _idem_, "The Faith of Israel", p.360. Cf. also Skehan, "The Structure", p.154, who similarly notes that such a concept as that of the heavenly assembly was not without its difficulty for the pious Jew living in a predominantly polytheistic world.
91   Würthwein, "Der Ursprung", pp.1-16.
92   _Ibid._, pp.10ff.
93   Hesse, "Wurzelt die prophetische Gerichtsrede", pp.46f.
94   Westermann, _Basic Forms_, p.78.
95   _Ibid._, pp.78f.
96   Cf. Eichrodt, _Der Heilige_, p.26; Wildberger, _Jesaja_, p.16; von Rad, _Old Testament Theology_, ii, p.151; _idem_, _Deuteronomy_, p.138. The purpose of the Deuteronomic law may originally have been to restrict the authority of the father over his family by requiring him to obtain the sanction of elders before bringing punishment upon his children. Cf. Clements, "The Relation of Children", p.196.
97   It is possible, however, that the words "glutton and drunkard" are to be regarded simply as additional evidence to ensure conviction. See Phillips, _Ancient Israel's Criminal Law_, pp.80f.

98   Cf. Cheyne, The Prophecies, i, p.2, who suggests that Yahweh is here speaking "rather in sorrow than in anger". Von Loewenclau, "Zur Auslegung", p.296, points out that the use of the word ^cammî is significant in this context, for if the oracle were based on the Deuteronomic provision, and if Yahweh were here seen in terms of a father who brought an accusation against his stubborn son, thus subjecting him to the severe punishment prescribed in that law, the prophet would surely have portrayed Yahweh as being separated from his people (cf. Hos. 1:9), and he would hardly have referred to them by the term ^cammî. Cf. also Vriezen, "Essentials", p.128, who notes that Isaiah sometimes uses the phrase "this people" (hā^cām hazzeh) in order to create a sense of distance between Yahweh and Israel (Is. 6:10; 8:6, 11f. etc.).

99   Driver, Deuteronomy, p.248; Wright, "Deuteronomy", p.462.

100   Eissfeldt, "Sohnespflichten", pp.39-47. Eissfeldt discusses, among other texts, the Keret legend, dating from the middle of the second millennium B.C., where a son's duty to honour his parents is particularly emphasised.

101   Von Loewenclau, "Zur Auslegung", p.307. For the wisdom background of these verses, see also Whedbee, Isaiah and Wisdom, pp.26ff.; Schlisske, Gottessöhne, pp.177-9.

102   Whedbee, Isaiah and Wisdom, pp.39-41; Wildberger, Jesaja, pp.14f.

103   Wildberger, loc. cit.

104   Cf. Oesterley, Proverbs, p.6.

105   Whedbee, Isaiah and Wisdom, pp.38f.

106   Ibid., pp.41f.; Wildberger, Jesaja, p.15.

107   Von Loewenclau, "Zur Auslegung", p.302.

Notes to Chapter Three
THE ACQUISITION OF LAND (Is. 5:8-10)

1   Cf., e.g., Neufeld, "The Emergence", pp.45ff.

2   Although there is no definite information in the Old Testament regarding the rate of interest charged in Israel, it is known that in Babylon during the first dynasty it was about 20-25% on money and about 33.3% on grain. Cf. Driver and Miles, The Babylonian Laws, i, p.176. Leemans, "The Rate of Interest", pp.32f., notes that this rate of interest was not

unduly high, since in a land as agriculturally productive as Babylonia, the farmer would have had a good return on his crop. In Assyria, it appears that the lender had a free hand in determining the rate which he wished the borrower to pay, but as a rule, it may be said that the interest on money ranged between 20% and 80% per annum, and the interest on grain might be as high as 50% per annum. Cf. Mendelsohn, Legal Aspects of Slavery, pp.10f.

3   CH§ 48 protects the debtor in the case of crop-failure (due to flood or drought) by stipulating that, in such circumstances, the debtor was to be excused from paying interest for that year. See Maloney, "Usury and Restrictions", pp.5f.

4   Mendelsohn, "Slavery in the O.T.", pp.384f., notes that of all the ancient law codes, the Old Testament alone mentions the case of self-sale or voluntary slavery. This does not mean, however, that this phenomenon was unknown elsewhere in the ancient Near East. See, further, Mendelsohn, "Slavery in the Ancient Near East", pp.78f.

5   A similar right was accorded the creditor in Babylonian and Assyrian law. Cf. Driver and Miles, The Babylonian Laws, i, pp.208-21; idem, The Assyrian Laws, pp.274ff.

6   Cf. Falk, Hebrew Law, p.102; Neufeld, "Self-help", pp.292f.

7   It appears that this prohibition was unique among the countries of the ancient Near East. See Gamoran, "The Biblical Law", pp.127f.

8   Cf. Driver, Deuteronomy, pp.266f.

9   According to Mendelsohn, the basic supply source of slavery in Israel, as in the ancient Near East generally, was the defaulting debtor. Cf. Slavery in the Ancient Near East, p.23.

10   Cf. Neufeld, "The Prohibitions", p.358, who comments: "The prohibition of interest which is resorted to for the protection of the poor and the needy is, in fact, a benefit only if the needy are sure to obtain a loan without interest, a circumstance generally overlooked".

11   Cf. North, "The Biblical Jubilee", p.333, who notes that the prohibition against lending at interest "could be a cruel restriction, since it practically closes off the access of the unfortunate to the capital needed for putting them on their feet again".

12   Cf. Stein, "The Laws on Interest", pp.168f.; Falk, Hebrew Law, pp.99f.; de Vaux, Ancient Israel, p.170. There is evidence to indicate that the Jews at Elephantine in the sixth century

B.C. lent to each other at an interest rate of 60% per annum. See Cowley, Aramaic Papyri, nos. 10-11, pp.29-35.

13   Cf. Gamoran, "The Biblical Law", pp.133f.

14   One possible exception is Neh. 5:11, but the text here is difficult. MT reads ומאת הכסף "and a hundredth part of the money". However, it is generally recognised that an interest rate of 1% per annum would be too small. It is possible that the reference is to the rate of interest charged per month, in which case it would amount to 12% per annum. But the most probable solution is that the word מאת should be emended to read מַשָּׁאת "debt". Cf. Rudolph, Esra und Nehemia, p.130. See also the discussion by Neufeld, "The Rate of Interest", pp.197ff.

15   It is probable that the creditor would either have taken the pledge by consent at the time the loan was made, or else he could seize the pledge from the borrower when the debt was overdue. Cf. Neufeld, "Inalienability", pp.34f.

16   Ibid., pp.33ff.; de Vaux, Ancient Israel, pp.171f.

17   It may be noted that this practice would have had clear parallels in Nuzi in the so-called ditennūtu documents which describe a procedure whereby the creditor lent money to the borrower on the condition that the latter grant him a part of his real estate as security for the loan. The creditor would have had possession but not ownership of the property, and he would have been entitled to the usufruct of the land for the duration of the loan. For a discussion of the ditennūtu documents, see Speiser, "New Kirkuk Documents", pp.350ff.; Clay, The Tenure of Land, pp.26-9; Steele, Nuzi Real Estate, pp.44-9; Mendelsohn Slavery in the Ancient Near East, pp.29-32. Mendelsohn, "On Slavery in Alalakh", pp.66f., notes that a similar system existed in Alalakh, where a pledge was taken as surety, and where the use of the pledge was considered as equivalent to the interest due on the loan. Similarly, in Assyria, loans were granted on security, and there are cases where houses and fields were given as a pledge, and in order to offset the interest on the loan, the creditor was entitled to the usufruct of the land. Cf. Mendelsohn, Legal Aspects, pp.15f. It may also be noted that CH§§ 49-51 envisages a case where the creditor takes over land which had been pledged for a loan, and takes his payment from the crops which the land would yield.

18   There is evidence that in Nuzi, where sale of real estate was also under strict control, tenants who had been forced to sell their property through economic hardship had evolved an ingenious method of legal evasion. Since property could be

passed on only to the nearest relatives of the tenant, the purchaser became, for legal purposes, the "son" of the seller, and by being incorporated into the family in this way, he obtained the full inheritance rights. Such cases fell officially into the category of "sale-adoptions" (mārūtu). Cf. Cross, Movable Property, pp.4f. These "sale-adoptions" were, therefore, a method of circumventing the regulations concerning the non-transferability of land, and they must not be confused with the "real-adoptions" which are also found at Nuzi. See Steele, Nuzi Real Estate, pp.14f. Gordon, The Living Past, pp.164-6, notes that some citizens in Nuzi had themselves "adopted" by numerous families, and in this way were able to accumulate vast tracts of land. It appears that in Mari, also, patrimony could not theoretically be transferred other than by inheritance, and so various means were contrived to circumvent the rule. Malamat, "Mari and the Bible", pp.147f., draws attention to one document from Mari in which, in order to obtain land, Yarim-Addu had to go through the legal fiction of becoming a "son" of the house of Awin. That Yarim-Addu was no more than a fictional brother of the sons of Awin is clear from another document in which his real father's name is given as Yapḫa. In Ugarit, too, there is evidence of fictional adoption, for one document describes how a widow "adopted" a son who brought five hundred shekels into her house. It is clear that this money was really his payment for the real estate received, since the property was conferred to him and his descendants for ever (PRU, iii, 1955, pp.64f., 303f.).

19   Cf. Daube, Studies, pp.44f.; Neufeld, "Ius Redemptionis", pp.34f.

20   The Law of Eshnunna (§ 39) similarly stipulated that if someone had been forced through poverty to sell his house he would retain the right to redeem it (ANET, p.163).

21   Cf. Gordon, "Sabbatical Cycle", p.81. Alt, "The Origins", p.128, n.118, suggests that the institution of the fallow year probably dates from an early period.

22   Sarna, "Zedekiah's Emancipation", pp.143-9, claims that the narrative of Jer. 34 reflects the Deuteronomic law of manumission (Deut. 15:12-18), although it designates the release by the term deror (Jer. 34:8, 15, 17), a word which occurs in the provisions connected with the Jubilee rather than with the Sabbath year (cf. Lev. 25:10). For a further discussion of the connection between Jer. 34 and the laws of manumission, see David, "The Manumission", pp.63ff.; Kessler, "The Law of

Manumission", pp.105ff.

23   Josephus testifies to the observance of the Sabbath year in the time of Alexander the Great (Ant. 11.8.6), and also in the period of the Hasmonaeans and the Herods (Ant. 13.8.1; 14.16.2). For a discussion of the references in Josephus, see North, "Maccabean Sabbath Years", pp.501ff.

24   The evidence for the existence of the Sabbath year in the post-exilic period is discussed by Wacholder, "The Calendar", pp.153ff.

25   A different interpretation of the text has been offered by North, Sociology, pp.32f., 185-7; and "Yâd in the Shemmitta-Law", pp.196-9, who argues that the law should rather be taken to refer to the return of pledged objects which had been taken by the creditor at the time of the loan. However, there is no reason to suppose that the law of šᵉmittāh was limited to any one particular kind of debt, or only to those debts in which a pledge had been taken as a form of security. Cf. Neufeld, "Socio-Economic Background", pp.61f.

26   CH§ 117 stipulates that the defaulting debtor was to be released from slavery after three years regardless of the amount of the debt. Mendelsohn, "Slavery in the O.T.", p.387, claims that it is doubtful whether this law was ever enforced, since there are many documents from Babylonia which attest the selling of people to the creditor, but none which mention their release after three years.

27   Cf. Ginzberg, "Studies", pp.348f.

28   Cf. Phillips, Ancient Israel's Criminal Law, p.77, who comments: "Provided a slave felt well treated, there was no point in exchanging security without freedom for freedom without security".

29   So, e.g., van der Ploeg, "Studies", p.169.

30   So, e.g., Horst, "Das Eigentum", pp.213f.

31   It is not certain whether the Jubilee was intended to be observed on the forty-ninth year or on the fiftieth. On the one hand, Lev. 25:8f. stipulates that the Jubilee was to be held on the seventh Sabbath year, but on the other hand, Lev. 25:10f. designates the Jubilee as the fiftieth year, and this seems to be supported by Lev. 25:18-22 which implies the existence of two successive fallows. For a detailed discussion of the problem, see North, Sociology, pp.109ff.

32   Cf., e.g., Elliger, Leviticus, pp.347ff.

33   So, e.g., Jirku, "Das israelitische Jobeljahr", p.178; Noth, Leviticus, pp.184f.; Rabinowitz, "A Biblical Parallel", p.95.

Notes to Chapter Three

34   Cf., e.g., Weber, Ancient Judaism, pp.71f.; Ginzberg, "Studies", p.368; de Vaux, Ancient Israel, pp.175-7.
35   Cf. Alexander, "A Babylonian Year", pp.75-9; Lewy, "The Biblical Institution", pp.21ff.
36   Cf., e.g., Wildberger, "Israel", pp.414f. The two passages which are thought to refer to the provision of the Jubilee are Ezek. 46:16-18 and Is. 61:1-4. In his idealized scheme for the reconstructed theocracy, Ezekiel notes that the prince can give the land as a gift to one of his subjects and that the recipient shall possess it until the year of release (deror). But although this passage probably reflects the provisions connected with the Jubilee, it cannot be regarded as evidence to support the historical observance of the institution, since Ezekiel's directions were clearly intended to have a future reference. In Is. 61:1-4, the prophet envisages a proclamation of liberty (deror) to the captives, but this reference is too obscure to provide any positive link with the Jubilee legislation. Cf. Westbrook, "Jubilee Laws", p.210.
37   Cf. Neufeld, "The Emergence", pp.31ff.
38   Whether 1 Sam. 8:10ff. is to be regarded as an authentic description of semi-feudal Canaanite society as it existed during the time of Samuel himself (cf. Mendelsohn, "Samuel's Denunciation", pp.17ff.), or whether it is a later reflection of the actual experience of the ways of the kings in Israel and Judah (cf. Clements, "The Deuteronomistic Interpretation", pp.398ff.), need not concern us here, but it may be taken for granted that the monarchial administration of David and Solomon did include many Canaanite features such as those enlisted in this passage.
39   Alt, "Der Anteil", pp.359f., suggests that both Abiathar, the priest (1 Kings 2:26f.), and Amaziah, the chief of the priesthood of Bethel (Am. 7:14-17), may have been granted property by the king as a fief. This custom of bestowing crown-lands to high officials was by no means uncommon in the ancient Near East. Mendelsohn, "Samuel's Denunciation", pp. 18f., points out that the Canaanite city-states had at their disposal professional warriors who received crown-lands for their service to the king. Similarly, in documents from Nuzi, there is a reference to an officer called the ḫalsuḫlu, whose duty seems to have been the assignment of crown-lands to some of the king's subjects. Cf. Lewy, "The Nuzian Feudal System", pp.7-9. In Babylonia, too, cases are recorded where the king gave his officials property as a reward for their services. See Clay,

The Tenure of Land, pp.11f.

40   Cf. Henrey, "Land Tenure", pp.11f. The precise meaning of the word ḥopšî is disputed, but Gray, "Feudalism", pp.54f., suggests that the term may have been used to refer to a class set apart for military service, and as such enjoying certain privileges which were usually associated with the feudal system. Albright, "Canaanite ḥapši", pp.106-8, argues that the primary meaning of the word is "a serf attached to the land", but that it later developed the meaning "peasant landholder, freeholder". For a further discussion of the term, see Mendelsohn, "The Canaanite Term", pp.36-9.

41   So, e.g., Aharoni, The Land, pp.323f. For a different view, however, see Yadin, "Ancient Judaean Weights", pp.17-25, who dates the ostraca in the time of Menahem.

42   It is probable that the preposition l^e in the formula refers to the recipient of the goods. Yadin, however, has suggested that the preposition l^e signifies the owner (and hence the sender, not the receiver) of the wine/oil in question. The formula would then be translated: "In the tenth year: From X (i.e. the main landowners) belonging to (l^e) Y (i.e. the sub-tenants)". See Yadin, "Recipients or Owners", pp.184-7. However, this interpretation involves certain difficulties. Cf. Rainey, "Administration", pp.62f.; idem, "The Samaria Ostraca", pp.32ff.; Aharoni, "The Samaria Ostraca", pp.67ff.

43   The places identified on the ostraca can all be located in the vicinity of Samaria. This geographical distribution would be difficult to understand if the places of origin were the personal estates of the recipients, since it is not likely that all the officials would have had their ancestral estates within the vicinity of the capital. See Mettinger, Solomonic State Officials, p.92.

44   Mendelsohn, "On Corvée Labor", pp.33f., cites a Hebrew letter from the seventh century B.C. which, if his interpretation of it is correct, may be regarded as extra-biblical evidence for the existence of the corvée in Israel. See also Talmon, "The New Hebrew Letter", pp.29ff.

45   In fact, the question as to whether Solomon imposed corvée on the Israelite citizens is problematic, for 1 Kings 9:22 suggests that the Israelites were exempt from this service, but this appears to be contradicted by the statements in 1 Kings 5:27; 11:28. Attempts have been made to reconcile these apparently conflicting statements by distinguishing between mas ^{c}ôbēd, permanent serfdom, which applied to the non-

Israelites, and mas, an occasional, ad hoc, regimentation, which did not involve the status of serfdom, but to which the Israelites were occasionally subjected. See, e.g., Mendelsohn, "State Slavery", pp.16f.; idem, Slavery in the Ancient Near East, pp.96-9.

46   Mendelsohn, "On Corvée Labor", p.33, suggests that the census ordered by the king in 2 Sam. 24:1-9 was undertaken for the threefold purpose of taxation, military service and corvée labour.

47   So, e.g., Mettinger, Solomonic State Officials, pp.70ff.

48   Cf. Noth, "Das Krongut", pp.212f.

49   Alt, "Der Anteil", pp.361-3, has argued that both transactions are to be understood in the light of Canaanite customs, since in neither case was the seller an Israelite.

50   Cf. Welten, "Naboths Weinberg", p.24. Seebass, "Der Fall Naboth", p.482, suggests that Elijah's words to Ahab, "Have you killed and also (wegam) taken possession?" (1 Kings 21:19) should be understood as an ironical retort on the part of the prophet: normally, the murderer would have forfeited his possession to the king, but in this case, the murderer himself had actually taken possession. However, Andersen, "The Socio-Juridical Background", pp.46ff., claims that the absence of any other clear example of the reversion to the crown of a convicted criminal's property makes this conclusion doubtful. He therefore suggests that Naboth was, in fact, executed for failing to carry through the agreed sale of his property to Ahab, and that it was for this reason that his land reverted to the crown after his death. But this is simply conjectural, and the most probable solution is that Ahab's "taking possession" of the vineyard does reflect a practice whereby the king "inherited" (yāraš) the property of a convicted offender. This practice seems to have been prevalent elsewhere in the ancient Near East. Rainey, "The Kingdom", pp.116f., notes that a custom existed in Ugarit whereby the king could dispose of property belonging to a guilty party as he saw fit. A similar practice is also attested in Alalakh; see Wiseman, The Alalakh Tablets, no.17.

51   This is, perhaps, implied by the phrase mišpaṭ hammelek in 1 Sam. 8:9 which may refer to the rights or prerogatives of the king. Similarly, in 1 Sam. 10:25, the phrase mišpaṭ hammelukāh probably refers to special statutes governing royal power.

52   Cf. Noth, "Das Krongut", p.212.

53   Cf. Östborn, Tōrā, pp.54ff. For a major review of this question see, most recently, Whitelam, The Just King, which appeared after the present study was completed.

54   Cf. Mendelsohn, "Authority and Law", pp.32f.

55   Alt, "Der Anteil", pp.353ff. See also Donner, "Die soziale Botschaft", pp.244f.

56   This is particularly evident in Micah's condemnation of those who devised methods of acquiring the property of others (Mic. 2:1-5), for here the prophet's threats were obviously aimed at the prosperous upper classes. Cf. Alt, "Micha 2, 1-5", pp.376f.

57   Alt, "Der Anteil", pp.364f.

58   This unit is unlike the preceding strophes in form and substance. Here, the threat is addressed in the second person to a particular group in the community, namely, those who issued decrees which robbed the helpless of their rights, whereas in the preceding section the accusations are of a more general nature and addressed to the people as a whole. Consequently, Is. 10:1-4 is either regarded as an isolated oracle of Isaiah (Skinner), or is attached to the series of woes in Is. 5:8-24 (Kaiser, Wildberger).

59   Hentschke, Satzung und Setzender, pp.11ff.

60   Ibid., pp.19f. Wildberger, Jesaja, p.198, suggests that the ḥōqᵉqîm were, in fact, royal officials. Cf. also Fohrer, Jesaja, i, pp.90f.

61   Cf. Procksch, Jesaia I, p.107; Kaiser, Isaiah 1-12, p.70; Fohrer, Jesaja, i, p.91; Wildberger, Jesaja, p.198.

62   Falk, Hebrew Law, p.26.

63   Cf. Victor, "A Note", pp.358-61.

64   Whedbee, Isaiah and Wisdom, pp.93ff.

65   Gerstenberger, "The Woe-Oracles", pp.249ff.

66   Wolff, Amos the Prophet, pp.17ff.

67   Ibid., pp.24f.

68   Wanke, "אוי und הוי", pp.215-8.

69   Wolff, Amos the Prophet, pp.25-30; cf. also Gerstenberger, "The Woe-Oracles", pp.260-2.

70   Cf. Janzen, " 'Ašrê", pp.220f.

71   Wolff, Amos the Prophet, pp.31f.

72   Cf. Westermann, Basic Forms, pp.190ff.

73   Cf. Janzen, Mourning Cry; Clifford, "The Use of Hôy", pp.458-64; Williams, "The Alas-Oracles", pp.75-91; Kraus, "hôj als profetische Leichenklage", pp.15-46.

74   Gerstenberger, "The Woe-Oracles", p.262.

75   For what follows, see Fey, Amos und Jesaja, pp.59-61.

76   Cf. Fichtner, "Die 'Umkehrung' ", cols.459-66.

Notes to Chapter Four
THE ADMINISTRATION OF JUSTICE (Is. 1:21-6)

1   Cf. Fey, Amos und Jesaja, p.64.

2   Cf. Wildberger, Jesaja, p.58; Kaiser, Isaiah 1-12, p.19.

3   Cf. Duhm, Jesaia, p.13, who suggests that these verses are dependent on the thought of Deutero- and Trito-Isaiah (cf. Is. 52:3ff.; 59:17-20; 61:8). For a different view, however, cf. Kissane, Isaiah, i, p.15.

4   Cf. Clements, Exodus, p.148.

5   Cf., e.g., Wildberger, Jesaja, p.61.

6   For a general discussion of the king's legislative powers, cf. de Vaux, Ancient Israel, pp.150-2.

7   Cf. Köhler, "Justice in the Gate", pp.163-5.

8   Cf. Phillips, Ancient Israel's Criminal Law, p.21.

9   The words kî lākem hammišpāṭ in Hos. 5:1 are ambiguous, since they might conceivably mean that judgement (mišpāṭ) will be passed on the king (cf. NEB). But it is more probable that the rendering of the RSV ("for the judgment pertains to you") reflects the proper meaning of MT, in which case Hosea is reproaching the king for neglecting his judicial responsibilities. Cf. the discussion by Mays, Hosea, pp.79f.

10   It is possible that other factors, in addition to David's neglect of his judicial responsibility, had precipitated Absalom's abortive rebellion against him. Weingreen, "The Rebellion", pp.263-6, suggests (partly on the basis of a Rabbinic comment in the Midrash) that behind the rebellion lay a widespread disillusionment with David's general ruthlessness such as that exemplified in his brutal disposal of Uriah.

11   Cf. von Rad, Deuteronomy, pp.117f.

12   The terms used in the Hebrew to designate these cultic and civil matters are dᵉbar-yhwh and dᵉbar-hammelek respectively (2 Chron. 19:11). Macholz, "Zur Geschichte", pp.325-7, claims that these expressions should not be interpreted as distinguishing sacral matters from the profane, since the line of demarcation between these categories would not always have been easy to draw. Rather, the terms should be understood as referring to those cases in which, due to lack of evidence, the decision was rendered by Yahweh (through the

oath, ordeal or lot), and those cases which could be decided by the king himself or his delegated official.

13   Cf. Bach, "Josaphat", cols.858f. Wellhausen, Prolegomena, p.191, argued that the attribution of the reorganisation to Jehoshaphat was simply due to the fact that his name meant "Yahweh is judge".

14   Albright, "The Judicial Reform", pp.61-82.

15   Cf. Macholz, "Zur Geschichte", pp.333ff.

16   Phillips, Ancient Israel's Criminal Law, pp.18-20.

17   Cf. Knierim, "Exodus 18", pp.169ff. Van der Ploeg, "Les chefs", pp.40-5, claims that the śar is the one who has the authority to issue commands, especially in a military capacity. He draws attention to Dan. 10:20 where the guardian angels are designated by the term śārîm, presumably because in the popular imagination they were conceived as commanders of celestial armies or as commanding human armies in battle.

18   Phillips, Ancient Israel's Criminal Law, pp.18-20.

19   Cf., e.g., McKay, "Exodus XXIII 1-3, 6-8", pp.316f.

20   Schwarz, " 'Begünstige nicht...'?", p.100, has argued that the phrase lō'-tiśśā' pᵉnê-dāl in Lev. 19:15b should be interpreted in the sense of "showing partiality against" rather than "showing partiality towards", and that the law is a warning against any tendency to be prejudiced against the poor. But this attempt to explain the verse is unnecessary, for the point of this law, like that of Ex. 23:3, is that one must not allow any feeling of pity or compassion towards the poor to influence one's judgement.

21   van Leeuwen, Le Développement, p.12.

22   For a discussion of the various occurrences of the word "elder" (zāqēn) in the Old Testament, cf. van der Ploeg, "Les Anciens", pp.175ff.

23   Cf. Pedersen, Israel, i-ii, p.36.

24   Wolf, "Traces", pp. 98-101, notes that the terms "men of Israel" and "elders" are occasionally used interchangeably in the Old Testament (cf. Josh. 24:1f., 19, 21), and he suggests that the two expressions were essentially synonymous. He also draws attention to the fact that there were seventy-seven elders in Succoth (Judg. 8:14) and suggests that this number would probably be large enough to represent the entire free male population of the town. However, Wolf fails to note that included in this number are the śārîm as well as the elders of Succoth. Moreover, it is unwise to draw any far-reaching conclusion from the single reference in Judg. 8:14, since this is

the only indication in the Old Testament of the number of elders in a specific town.

25   Phillips, Ancient Israel's Criminal Law, pp.17f.

26   Cf. Bornkamm, "πρεσβυς", p.655. Jacobsen, "Primitive Democracy", pp.165f., points out that the assemblies at Uruk in the time of Gilgamesh consisted of a body of elders who possessed certain advisory powers, and he argues on the basis of the Sumerian terms abba ("father") and abba uru ("town fathers") that they probably formed the heads of the various large families which made up the population of the town. Cf. Evans, "Ancient Mesopotamian Assemblies", pp.7-11.

27   McKenzie, "The Elders", p.538.

28   Phillips, Ancient Israel's Criminal Law, pp.151f., argues that the purpose of the tenth commandment in its original form was to ensure the continuance of the democratic nature of the administration of justice in Israel by prohibiting the seizure of a neighbour's house. However, this view is unlikely, for Phillips admits that it is difficult to get the verb ḥāmad to mean "seize", and he is therefore forced to conclude that in the original commandment a verb other than ḥāmad was used.

29   It is generally acknowledged that the narrative as it stands comes from the late P source, but the vividness of the account may suggest that the author here incorporated an early tradition. Cf. von Rad, Genesis (revised edition, 1972), pp.246f., 249f. Lehmann, "Abraham's Purchase", pp.15-18, notes that certain features in the narrative of Gen. 23 are paralleled in Hittite legal texts dating from the second millennium B.C., and on the basis of this observation he suggests an early date for the biblical narrative. It is doubtful, however, whether Abraham's purchase of the cave and field of Machpelah should be understood against a background of Hittite legal practice. Cf. Tucker, "The Legal Background", pp.77-9.

30   Speiser, "'Coming' and 'Going'", pp.20-3, argues that the phrase refers only to the "city fathers or elders", i.e. to those qualified to sit in the assembly at the gate. He draws attention to the parallel expression in Gen. 34:24, "all who went out of the gate of his city" (kol-yōṣeʾê šaʿar ʿîrô), and suggests that this phrase refers to all who go out in battle, namely the young, able-bodied men of the community who were capable of bearing arms. However, Evans,"'Coming' and 'Going'", pp.28-33, argues that the difference between the two expressions should not be over-emphasised. The phrase "all who went out of the gate of his city" in Gen. 34:24 seems to refer to every male

(kol-zākār), and since these did not include children (v.29), it is probable that the males in question were those who had reached the age of puberty and who had therefore been circumcised (vv.22, 24). Thus the expressions "to go out of" or "go in by" the city gate referred to those who could be regarded as full citizens.

31   Cf. Speiser, Genesis, p.170, who describes Abraham's position as that of a "long-term resident, but one lacking the normal privileges of a citizen (cf. xii 10, xix 9), notably, the right to own land".

32   Cf. von Rad, Genesis, p.247, who notes that Abraham's position "would be significantly changed if he were now to possess a piece of ground, even though quite small".

33   For a discussion of the various activities which were carried out "at the gate", cf. Evans, "'Gates' and 'Streets'", pp.1-12.

34   Cf. Köhler, "Justice in the Gate", pp.152f.

35   Cf. Kramer, History, p.94.

36   ANET, p.178. A similar concern for the poor is found in Ugaritic literature, for here Dan'el is depicted as taking his seat by the threshing floor "to judge the cause of the widow and adjudicate the cause of the fatherless" (ANET, p.151), and in another text, Keret is admonished by his son Yassib to secure justice for the oppressed (ANET, p.149). Hammershaimb, "On the Ethics", pp.79ff., points out that the words used in these texts to designate the widow and the orphan (Ug. almnt; ytm) are identical with those used in the Old Testament to denote the same group (Heb. 'almānāh; yātôm), and that the verb used for "securing justice" is the same in both cases (Ug. tpt; Heb. šāpat). He therefore concludes that the concern for the widow and orphan found in the prophetic literature is of Canaanite origin. This is unlikely, however, for as Fensham, "Widow, Orphan", pp.129-39, points out, the care of the widow and orphan was such a common concern throughout the ancient Near East from the earliest times that it is quite unnecessary to speak of a borrowing of one culture from another in this regard. Moreover, it is probable that concern for the widow and orphan was felt by the Hebrews in the nomadic or semi-nomadic period, i.e. before the settlement in Canaan. Cf. von Waldow, "Social Responsibility", pp.184-7.

37   Although the passage as it stands is comparatively late (P), it is generally agreed that vv.8-11, which include a formal statement of the law of inheritance in Israel, reflect an older

tradition. Cf. Noth, Numbers, p.211.

38   Job 42: 13-15 seems to be an instance of inheritance by daughters despite the fact that there were male heirs, but this probably represents a later custom.

39   The locus classicus here is Lam. 5:3 which reads y^{e}tômîm hāyînû 'ēn 'āb.

40   Cf. van Leeuwen, Le Développement, pp.24f.

41   Cf., further, my article, "Inheritance Rights".

42   Cf. Whedbee, Isaiah and Wisdom, pp.108f.

43   Cf. Wolff, Amos the Prophet. The Man and his Background, p.83.

44   Whedbee, Isaiah and Wisdom, p.109.

45   Cf. van Leeuwen, Le Développement, pp.153ff.

46   Kuschke, "Arm und reich", pp.48ff., argues that the words used to characterise this attitude towards poverty are rûš, ḥāsēr, and miskēn, but that in those contexts where feelings of pity or compassion are expressed towards the poor, the words used are 'ebyôn, dal and ʿānî. However, it is doubtful whether such a sharp distinction should be drawn between the two sets of expressions. Cf. van der Ploeg, "Les Pauvres", pp.236ff.

47   One possible exception to this may be found in Prov. 23:10, for the word ʿôlām here is sometimes emended to 'almānāh, and the verse would then be rendered: "Do not remove the landmark of the widow or enter the fields of the orphan". The emendation would certainly provide a good parallel to y^{e}tômîm in v.10b and may be supported by the corresponding passage in Amenemope. But these reasons in themselves are not sufficient to warrant emending the verse, and the reading of MT should therefore be preserved. Cf. McKane, Proverbs, p.380.

48   Wolff, Amos the Prophet, p.83.

49   McKane, Proverbs, pp.485, 512, argues that these contrasting views towards bribery are to be accounted for on the supposition of a reinterpretation of the vocabulary of old wisdom. Cf., further, McKane, Prophets and Wise Men, p.65. However, it is more likely that the differences are due to the fact that various groups among the wise held different outlooks.

50   Fey, Amos und Jesaja, pp.57-9.

51   MT reads the plural ṣaddîqîm, but LXX and Vulg. suggest reading the singular ṣaddîq, presumably to correspond to the singular rāšāʿ in the first half of the verse.

52   According to Greenberg, "Some Postulates", pp.13ff., this absolute ban on composition for homicide is without

parallel in the laws of the ancient Near East. Cf., further, Greenberg, "Crimes and Punishments", p.738.

53   Cf. McKeating, "Sanctions", pp.59-61.

54   This is suggested by Ex. 21:22 which deals with compensation for the loss of an infant. See Clements, Exodus, p.138.

55   As McKeating, "The Development", pp.55f., observes, the law prohibiting compensation for homicide (Num. 35:31) comes from the priestly source, and since lawgivers would not legislate against offences which were not being perpetrated, it is likely that, at least until the time of the exile, some continued to support the system of monetary payments in recompense for homicide.

Notes to Chapter Five
CONCLUSION

1   Even Eichrodt, who had made the covenant the structural centre of his reconstruction of the theology of the Old Testament, was able to say of the prophets that the "concept of the covenant never proved adequate to the outpouring of the riches of their vision of God" (Theology, i, p.68).

2   Fensham, "Common Trends", pp.155-75; Hillers, Treaty-Curses, pp.43ff. Fensham also suggested that the curses preserved in Deut. 28 and Lev. 26 could be traced back to specific treaties in the ancient Near East. Cf., further, his article, "Malediction", pp.1-9. For the parallels between the curses of the Assyrian treaties and those of Deut. 28, see also Frankena, "The Vassal-Treaties", pp.122-54; Weinfeld, "Traces", pp.417-27.

3   Cf. McCarthy, Old Testament Covenant, p.58.

4   Hillers, Treaty-Curses, pp.86f.

5   Ibid., p.85.

6   Cf. Clements, Prophecy and Tradition, p.19, who observes: "The similarities are no more than may be expected in a situation where the general conditions of life, the possibilities of misfortune, and especially the nature and methods of warfare, were very similar throughout a large area. The similarity of the prophetic threats with treaty curses is explicable simply on the recognition that descriptions of evil

and misfortune were bound to show a considerable degree of similarity because all peoples were subject to essentially similar threats to life and security. There is nothing of a specifically covenantal, or treaty, character about this".
7   Cf. Scott, The Way of Wisdom, pp.129-32.

LIST OF ABBREVIATIONS

AER	American Ecclesiastical Review
An.Bib.	Analecta Biblica
ANET	Ancient Near Eastern Texts Relating to the Old Testament, ed. J.B. Pritchard, Princeton, 1950.
Ant.	Fl. Josephus, Antiquitates Judaicae
ARM	Archives royales de Mari, publiées sous la direction de A. Parrot et G. Dossin, Paris.
ATD	Das Alte Testament Deutsch
BA	The Biblical Archaeologist
BASOR	Bulletin of the American Schools of Oriental Research
BDB	F. Brown, S.R. Driver and C.A. Briggs, A Hebrew and English Lexicon of the Old Testament, Oxford, 1907.
Bib.Or.	Bibliotheca Orientalis
Bib.Zeit.	Biblische Zeitschrift
BKAT	Biblischer Kommentar, Altes Testament
BWANT	Beiträge zur Wissenschaft vom Alten und Neuen Testament
BZAW	Beihefte zur Zeitschrift für die alttestamentliche Wissenschaft
CBQ	Catholic Biblical Quarterly
Cent.B.	The Century Bible
CH	The Code of Hammurabi
Con.Bib.	Coniectanea Biblica
EvTh	Evangelische Theologie
Exp.T.	The Expository Times
G-K	A.E. Cowley, Gesenius' Hebrew Grammar as edited and enlarged by the late E. Kautzsch, 2nd edn., Oxford, 1910.
HAT	Handbuch zum Alten Testament
HTR	Harvard Theological Review
HUCA	Hebrew Union College Annual
IB	The Interpreter's Bible, ed. G.A. Buttrick et al., New York, 1952-7.
ICC	The International Critical Commentary
IDB	The Interpreter's Dictionary of the Bible, ed. G.A. Buttrick et al., New York, Nashville, 1962.

Abbreviations

IEJ	Israel Exploration Journal
ILR	Israel Law Review
JAOS	Journal of the American Oriental Society
JBL	Journal of Biblical Literature
JEA	Journal of Egyptian Archaeology
JNES	Journal of Near Eastern Studies
JNWSL	Journal of Northwest Semitic Languages
JPOS	Journal of the Palestine Oriental Society
JQR	Jewish Quarterly Review
JRH	Journal of Religious History
JSOT	Journal for the Study of the Old Testament
JTS	Journal of Theological Studies
KAT	Kommentar zum Alten Testament
KS	A. Alt, Kleine Schriften zur Geschichte des Volkes Israel (München, Vols. I, II, 1953; Vol. III, 1959).
LXX	The Septuagint
MT	The Massoretic Text
NEB	The New English Bible
Or. Ant.	Oriens Antiquus
OTL	Old Testament Library
OTS	Oudtestamentische Studiën
PEQ	Palestine Exploration Quarterly
PRU	Le Palais Royal d'Ugarit (Mission de Ras Shamra), ed. C.F.-A. Schaeffer, Paris, 1955.
RB	Revue Biblique
RGG	Die Religion in Geschichte und Gegenwart
RHPhR	Revue d'Histoire et de Philosophie religieuse
RIDA	Revue Internationale des Droits de l'Antiquité
RSV	The Revised Standard Version
RThPh	Revue de Théologie et de Philosophie
SBT	Studies in Biblical Theology
TDNT	Theological Dictionary of the New Testament (Eng. tr. by G.W. Bromiley of Theologisches Wörterbuch zum Neuen Testament), ed. G. Kittel (Vols. I-IV), G. Friedrich (Vols. V-IX).
ThZ	Theologische Zeitschrift
TLZ	Theologische Literaturzeitung
TWNT	Theologisches Wörterbuch zum Neuen Testament, ed. G. Kittel and G. Friedrich.
VT	Vetus Testamentum
VTS	Supplements to Vetus Testamentum
WMANT	Wissenschaftliche Monographien zum Alten und Neuen Testament

WuD	Wort und Dienst
ZAW	Zeitschrift für die alttestamentliche Wissenschaft
ZDPV	Zeitschrift des Deutschen Palästina-Vereins
ZThK	Zeitschrift für Theologie und Kirche

Bibliography

Aharoni, Y.

> The Land of the Bible: A Historical Geography (London, 1967; first published, Jerusalem, 1962; Eng. tr. from the Hebrew original by A.F. Rainey).

> "The Samaria Ostraca - An Additional Note", IEJ, xii, 1962, pp.67-9.

Albright, W.F.

> "Canaanite Ḥapši and Hebrew Ḥofsî Again", JPOS, vi, 1926, pp.106-8.

> "The Judicial Reform of Jehoshaphat", Alexander Marx Jubilee Volume (ed. S. Lieberman, New York, 1950), pp.61-82.

> "Some Canaanite-Phoenician Sources of Hebrew Wisdom", VTS, iii, 1955, pp.1-15.

> "Some Remarks on the Song of Moses in Deuteronomy XXXII", VT, ix, 1959, pp.339-46.

Alexander, J.B.

> "A Babylonian Year of Jubilee?", JBL, lvii, 1938, pp.75-9.

Alt, A.

> "Der Anteil des Königtums an der sozialen Entwicklung in den Reichen Israel und Juda", KS, iii, 1959, pp.348-72.

> "Micha 2, 1-5 ΓΗΣ ΑΝΑΔΑΣΜΟΣ in Juda", Interpretationes ad Vetus Testamentum pertinentes Sigmundo Mowinckel septuagenario missae (eds. N.A. Dahl and A.S. Kapelrud, Oslo, 1955), pp.13-23 (= KS, iii, 1959, pp.373-81).

> Die Ursprünge des israelitischen Rechts, Leipzig, 1934 (= KS, i, 1953, pp.278-332; Eng. tr. by R.A. Wilson, "The Origins of Israelite Law", Essays on Old Testament History and Religion, Oxford, 1966, pp. 81-132).

> "Die Weisheit Salomos", TLZ, lxxvi, 1951, cols.139-44 (= KS, ii, 1953, pp.90-9).

Amsler, S.

> "Le Thème du procès chez les prophètes d'Israël", RThPh[3], xxiv, 1974, pp.116-31.

Andersen, F.I.
"The Socio-Juridical Background of the Naboth Incident", JBL, lxxxv, 1966, pp.46-57.
Anderson, R.T.
"Was Isaiah a Scribe?", JBL, lxxix, 1960, pp.57-8.
Bach, R.
"Gottesrecht und weltliches Recht in der Verkündigung des Propheten Amos", Festschrift Günther Dehn (ed. W. Schneemelcher, Neukirchen, 1957), pp. 23-34.

"Josaphat", RGG³, iii, 1959, cols.858-9.
Baltzer, K.
Das Bundesformular, WMANT 4, Neukirchen, 1960 (Eng. tr. by D.E. Green, The Covenant Formulary, Oxford, 1971).
Bentzen, A.
Introduction to the Old Testament, i, Copenhagen, 1948.
Bergren, R.V.
The Prophets and the Law, HUCA Monograph Series 4, Cincinnati, 1974.
Beyerlin, W.
Herkunft und Geschichte der ältesten Sinaitraditionen, Tübingen, 1961 (Eng. tr. by S. Rudman, Origins and History of the Oldest Sinaitic Traditions, Oxford, 1965).
Blanchette, O.
"The Wisdom of God in Isaia", AER, cxlv, 1961, pp.413-23.
Boecker, H.J.
"Anklagereden und Verteidigungsreden im Alten Testament", EvTh, xx, 1960, pp.398-412.

Redeformen des Rechtslebens im Alten Testament, WMANT 14, Neukirchen, 1964.
Bornkamm, G.
"Die 'Ältesten' in der israelitisch-jüdischen Verfassungs-geschichte" in "πρεσβυς κτλ.", TWNT, vi, pp.655-61 (Eng. tr. "'Elders' in the Constitutional History of Israel and Judah", TDNT, vi, 1968, pp.655-61).
Bright, J.
"The Apodictic Prohibition: Some Observations", JBL, xcii, 1973, pp.185-204.

A History of Israel, OTL, London, 1960 (revised edition, 1972).
"Isaiah - I", Peake's Commentary on the Bible, eds. M. Black and H.H. Rowley (London, 1962), pp.489-515.

Bibliography

Cassuto, U.
> "The Song of Moses (Deuteronomy Chapter XXXII 1-43)" (originally published in 1938), Biblical and Oriental Studies, i, Jerusalem, 1973, pp.41-70 (Eng. tr. by I. Abrahams).

Causse, A.
> Du Groupe ethnique à la communauté religieuse: le problème sociologique de la religion d'Israël, Paris, 1937.

> "Les Prophètes et la crise sociologique de la religion d'Israël", RHPhR, xii, 1932, pp.97-140.

Cazelles, H.
> "Les Débuts de la sagesse en Israël", Les Sagesses du proche-orient ancien, Paris, 1963, pp.27-40.

Cheyne, T.K.
> The Prophecies of Isaiah, i, London, 1880.

Clay, R.
> The Tenure of Land in Babylonia and Assyria, London, 1938.

Clements, R.E.
> A Century of Old Testament Study, Guildford and London, 1976.

> "The Deuteronomistic Interpretation of the Founding of the Monarchy in 1 Sam. VIII", VT, xxiv, 1974, pp.398-410.

> Exodus, Cambridge Bible Commentary, Cambridge, 1972.

> Prophecy and Covenant, SBT[1] 43, London, 1965.

> Prophecy and Tradition, Oxford, 1975.

> "The Relation of Children to the People of God in the Old Testament", Baptist Quarterly, N.S., xxi, 1966, pp. 195-205.

Clifford, R.J.
> "The Use of Hôy in the Prophets", CBQ, xxviii, 1966, pp. 458-64.

Cowley, A.E.
> Aramaic Papyri of the Fifth Century B.C., Oxford, 1923.

Crenshaw, J.L.
> "The Influence of the Wise upon Amos. The 'Doxologies of Amos' and Job 5:9-16; 9:5-10", ZAW, lxxix, 1967, pp.42-52.

Cross, D.
> Movable Property in the Nuzi Documents, American Oriental Society, 10, New Haven, 1937.

Cross, F.M.
"The Council of Yahweh in Second Isaiah", JNES, xii, 1953, pp.274-7.
Daube, D.
"Direct and Indirect Causation in Biblical Law", VT, xi, 1961, pp.246-69.

"Rechtsgedanken in den Erzählungen des Pentateuchs", Von Ugarit nach Qumran, O. Eissfeldt Festschrift, eds. J. Hempel and L. Rost, BZAW 77, Berlin, 1958, pp.32-41.

Studies in Biblical Law, Cambridge, 1947.
David, M.
"The Manumission of Slaves under Zedekiah", OTS, v, 1948, pp.63-79.
Davies, E.W.
"Inheritance Rights and the Hebrew Levirate Marriage" (to be published, in two parts, in forthcoming issues of VT).
Delcor, M.
"Les attaches littéraires, l'origine et la signification de l'expression biblique 'Prendre à témoin le ciel et la terre'", VT, xvi, 1966, pp.8-25.
Donner, H.
"Die soziale Botschaft der Propheten im Lichte der Gesellschaftsordnung in Israel", Or.Ant., ii, 1963, pp. 229-45.
Driver, G.R.
The Assyrian Laws, Oxford, 1935 (with J.C. Miles).

The Babylonian Laws, i, Oxford, 1952 (with J.C. Miles).

"Hebrew Scrolls", JTS, N.S., ii, 1951, pp.17-30.
Driver, S.R.
A Critical and Exegetical Commentary on Deuteronomy, ICC, Edinburgh, 1895.
Duhm, B.
Das Buch Jesaia, HAT, III, 1, Göttingen, 1892.

Israels Propheten, Tübingen, second edition, 1922.

Die Theologie der Propheten, Bonn, 1875.
Dupont-Sommer, A.
Les Inscriptions araméennes de Sfiré (Stèles I et II), Paris, 1958.
Eichrodt, W.
"Covenant and Law", Interpretation, xx, 1966, pp.302-21.

Bibliography

Der Heilige in Israel, Die Botschaft des Alten Testaments XVII, 1, Stuttgart, 1960.

Theologie des Alten Testaments, i, Leipzig, 1933 (Eng. tr. by J.A. Baker from 6th German edition, Theology of the Old Testament, i, OTL, London, 1961).

Eissfeldt, O.
Einleitung in das Alte Testament, Tübingen, 1934 (Eng. tr. by P.R. Ackroyd from 3rd German edition, The Old Testament: An Introduction, Oxford, 1965).

Das Lied Moses Deuteronomium 32:1-43 und das Lehrgedicht Asaphs Psalm 78 samt einer Analyse der Umgebung des Mose-Liedes, Berichte über die Verhandlungen der Sächsischen Akademie der Wissenschaften zu Leipzig, civ, 5, Berlin, 1958.

"Sohnespflichten im alten Orient", Syria, xliii, 1966, pp. 39-47.

Elliger, K.
Leviticus, HAT, I, 4, Tübingen, 1966.

Evans, D.G.
"Ancient Mesopotamian Assemblies", JAOS, lxxviii, 1958, pp.1-11.

"'Coming' and 'Going' at the City Gate - A Discussion of Professor Speiser's Paper", BASOR 150 (April, 1958), pp. 28-33.

"'Gates' and 'Streets': Urban Institutions in Old Testament Times", JRH, ii, 1962, pp.1-12.

Falk, Z.W.
Hebrew Law in Biblical Times, Jerusalem, 1964.

Fensham, F.C.
"Common Trends in Curses of the Near Eastern Treaties and Kudurru-Inscriptions compared with Maledictions of Amos and Isaiah", ZAW, lxxv, 1963, pp.155-75.

"Father and Son as Terminology for Treaty and Covenant", Near Eastern Studies in Honor of W.F. Albright, ed. H. Goedicke, Baltimore, 1971, pp.121-35.

"Malediction and Benediction in Ancient Near Eastern Vassal-Treaties and the Old Testament", ZAW, lxxiv, 1962, pp.1-9.

"Widow, Orphan, and the Poor in Ancient Near Eastern

Legal and Wisdom Literature", JNES, xxi, 1962, pp.129-39.
Fey, R.
Amos und Jesaja, WMANT 12, Neukirchen, 1963.
Fichtner, J.
"Jesaja unter den Weisen", TLZ, lxxiv, 1949, cols.75-80.

"Die 'Umkehrung' in der prophetischen Botschaft. Eine Studie zu dem Verhältnis von Schuld und Gericht in der Verkündigung Jesajas", TLZ, lxxviii, 1953, cols.459-66.
Fohrer, G.
Das Buch Jesaja, i, Zürcher Bibelkommentare, Zürich-Stuttgart, 1960.

Einleitung in das Alte Testament, 10th ed. by E. Sellin, revised by G. Fohrer, Heidelberg, 1965 (Eng. tr. by D. Green, Introduction to the Old Testament, London, 1970).

"Jesaja 1 als Zusammenfassung der Verkündigung Jesajas", ZAW, lxxiv, 1962, pp.251-68.

"Remarks on Modern Interpretation of the Prophets", JBL, lxxx, 1961, pp.309-19.

"Tradition und Interpretation im Alten Testament", ZAW, lxxiii, 1961, pp.1-30.
Frankena, R.
"The Vassal-Treaties of Esarhaddon and the Dating of Deuteronomy", OTS, xiv, 1965, pp.122-54.
Gamoran, H.
"The Biblical Law against Loans on Interest", JNES, xxx, 1971, pp.127-34.
Gemser, B.
"The Rîb- or Controversy-Pattern in Hebrew Mentality", VTS, iii, 1955, pp.120-37.
Gerstenberger, E.
"Covenant and Commandment", JBL, lxxxiv, 1965, pp. 38-51.

Wesen und Herkunft des "apodiktischen Rechts", WMANT 20, Neukirchen, 1965.

"The Woe-Oracles of the Prophets", JBL, lxxxi, 1962, pp. 249-63.
Gevirtz, S.
"West-Semitic Curses and the Problem of the Origins of Hebrew Law", VT, xi, 1961, pp.137-58.

Bibliography

Ginzberg, E.
"Studies in the Economics of the Bible", JQR, N.S., xxii, 1932, pp.343-408.
Gordon, C.H.
The Living Past, New York, 1941.

"Sabbatical Cycle or Seasonal Pattern?", Orientalia, N.S., xxii, 1953, pp.79-81.
Gray, G.B.
A Critical and Exegetical Commentary on the Book of Isaiah (I-XXVII), ICC, Edinburgh, 1912.
Gray, J.
"Feudalism in Ugarit and Early Israel", ZAW, lxiv, 1952, pp.49-55.
Greenberg, M.
"Crimes and Punishments", IDB, i, 1962, pp.733-44.

"Some Postulates of Biblical Criminal Law", Yehezkel Kaufmann Jubilee Volume, ed. M. Haran, Jerusalem, 1960, pp.5-28.
Gunkel, H.
Einleitung in die Psalmen (completed by J. Begrich), Göttingen, 1933.

"Vergeltung", RGG^2, v, 1931, cols.1529-33.
Hammershaimb, E.
"On the Ethics of the Old Testament Prophets", VTS, vii, 1959, pp.75-101.
Harvey, J.
Le Plaidoyer prophétique contre Israël après la rupture de l'alliance, Paris and Montreal, 1967.

"Le 'rîb-pattern', réquisitoire prophétique sur la rupture de l'alliance", Biblica, xliii, 1962, pp.172-96.
Hempel, J.
Das Ethos des Alten Testaments, BZAW 67, 1938 (second revised edition, Berlin, 1964).
Henrey, K. H.
"Land Tenure in the Old Testament", PEQ, lxxxvi, 1954, pp.5-15.
Hentschke, R.
Satzung und Setzender: Ein Beitrag zur israelitischen Rechtsterminologie, BWANT V, 3, Stuttgart, 1963.
Herdner, A.
Corpus des tablettes en cunéiformes alphabétiques

découvertes à Ras Shamra-Ugarit de 1929 à 1939, Paris, 1963.

Heschel, A. J.
  The Prophets, New York, 1962.

Hesse, F.
  "Wurzelt die prophetische Gerichtsrede im israelitischen Kult?", ZAW, lxv, 1953, pp.45-53.

Hillers, D. R.
  Covenant: The History of a Biblical Idea, Baltimore, 1969.

  Treaty-Curses and the Old Testament Prophets, Bib.Or. 16, Rome, 1964.

Hoffmann, H. W.
  Die Intention der Verkündigung Jesajas, BZAW 136, Berlin, 1974.

Hölscher, G.
  Die Profeten, Leipzig, 1914.

Horst, F.
  "Das Eigentum nach dem Alten Testament", Kirche im Volk, ii, 1949, pp.87-101 (= Gottes Recht: Gesammelte Studien zum Recht im Alten Testament, ed. H.W. Wolff, München, 1961, pp.203-21).

Huffmon, H.B.
  "The Covenant Lawsuit in the Prophets", JBL, lxxviii, 1959, pp.285-95.

  "The Treaty Background of Hebrew Yāda^c", BASOR 181 (February, 1966), pp.31-7.

  "A Further Note on the Treaty Background of Hebrew Yāda^c", BASOR 184 (December, 1966), pp.36-8 (with S.B. Parker).

Jacobsen, T.
  "Primitive Democracy in Ancient Mesopotamia", JNES, ii, 1943, pp.159-72.

Janzen, W.
  "'Ašrê in the Old Testament", HTR, lviii, 1965, pp.215-26.

  Mourning Cry and Woe Oracle, BZAW 125, Berlin, 1972.

Jirku, A.
  "Das israelitische Jobeljahr", Reinhold-Seeberg-Festschrift, ed. W. Koepp, Leipzig, 1929, pp.169-79.

Kaiser, O.
  Der Prophet Jesaja 1-12, ATD 17, Göttingen, second edition, 1963 (Eng. tr. by R.A. Wilson, Isaiah 1-12, OTL,

London, 1972).

Kessler, M.
"The Law of Manumission in Jer 34", Bib. Zeit., N.F., xv, 1971, pp.105-8.

Kimbrough, S.T.
"Une Conception sociologique de la religion d'Israël: l'oeuvre d'Antonin Causse", RHPhR, xlix, 1969, pp.313-26.

Israelite Religion in Sociological Perspective. The Work of Antonin Causse, Wiesbaden, 1978.

Kissane, E.J.
The Book of Isaiah, i, Dublin, 1941.

Knierim, R.
"Exodus 18 und die Neuordnung der Mosaischen Gerichtsbarkeit", ZAW, lxxiii, 1961, pp.146-71.

Die Hauptbegriffe für Sünde im Alten Testament, Gütersloh, 1965.

Köhler, L.
Deuterojesaja (Jesaja 40-55) stilkritisch untersucht, BZAW 37, Giessen, 1923.

Die hebräische Rechtsgemeinde, Zürich, 1931 (Eng. tr. by P.R. Ackroyd, "Justice in the Gate" in Hebrew Man, London, 1956, pp.149-75; itself a translation of L. Köhler, Der hebräische Mensch, Tübingen, 1953).

"Sīg, sīgīm = Bleiglätte", ThZ, iii, 1947, pp.232-4.

Kramer, S.N.
History Begins at Sumer, London, 1958.

Kraus, H.J.
"hôj als profetische Leichenklage über das eigene Volk im 8. Jahrhundert", ZAW, lxxxv, 1973, pp.15-46.

Kuschke, A.
"Arm und reich im Alten Testament mit besonderer Berücksichtigung der nachexilischen Zeit", ZAW, lvii, 1939, pp.31-57.

Lagarde, P. de
Symmicta, i, Göttingen, 1877.

Langdon, S.
"The Treaty of Alliance between Ḫattušili, King of the Hittites, and the Pharaoh Ramesses II of Egypt", JEA, vi, 1920, pp.179-205 (with A.H. Gardiner).

Leemans, W. F.
"The Rate of Interest in Old-Babylonian Times", RIDA^2,

v, 1950, pp.7-34.

Leeuwen, C. van
Le Développement du sens social en Israël avant l'ère chrétienne, Studia Semitica Neerlandica, Assen, 1955.

Lehmann, M.R.
"Abraham's Purchase of Machpelah and Hittite Law", BASOR 129 (February, 1953), pp.15-18.

Lewy, H.
"The Nuzian Feudal System", Orientalia, N.S., xi, 1942, pp.1-40.

Lewy, J.
"The Biblical Institution of D^{e}rôr in the Light of Akkadian Documents", Eretz-Israel, v, 1958, pp.21-31.

Liebesny, H.
"Evidence in Nuzi Legal Procedure", JAOS, lxi, 1941, pp.130-42.

Limburg, J.
The Lawsuit of God in the Eighth-Century Prophets, unpublished dissertation, Union Theological Seminary, Virginia, 1969.

"The Root ריב and the Prophetic Lawsuit Speeches", JBL, lxxxviii, 1969, pp.291-304.

Lindblom, J.
Prophecy in Ancient Israel, Oxford, 1962.

"Wisdom in the Old Testament Prophets", VTS, iii, 1955, pp.192-204.

Loewenclau, I. von
"Zur Auslegung von Jesaja 1, 2-3", EvTh, xxvi, 1966, pp.294-308.

Lowth, R.
Isaiah: A New Translation, London, 1778.

Macholz, G.C.
"Zur Geschichte der Justizorganisation in Juda", ZAW, lxxxiv, 1972, pp.314-40.

"Die Stellung des Königs in der israelitischen Gerichtsverfassung", ZAW, lxxxiv, 1972, pp.157-82.

MacKenzie, R.A.F.
"The Formal Aspect of Ancient Near Eastern Law", The Seed of Wisdom: Essays in Honour of T.J. Meek, ed. W.S. McCullough, Toronto, 1964, pp.31-44.

Malamat, A.

"Mari and the Bible: Some Patterns of Tribal Organization and Institutions", JAOS, lxxxii, 1962, pp.143-50.

Maloney, R.P.

"Usury and Restrictions on Interest-Taking in the Ancient Near East", CBQ, xxxvi, 1974, pp.1-20.

Marshall, R.J.

"The Structure of Isaiah 1-12", Biblical Research, vii, 1962, pp.19-32.

Martin-Achard, R.

"Sagesse de Dieu et sagesse humaine chez Esaie", Maqqél Shâqédh: Hommage à Wilhelm Vischer, Montpellier, 1960, pp.137-44.

Mays, J.L.

Hosea: A Commentary, OTL, London, 1969.

McCarthy, D. J.

"Covenant in the Old Testament: The Present State of Inquiry", CBQ, xxvii, 1965, pp.217-40.

"Notes on the Love of God in Deuteronomy and the Father-Son Relationship between Yahweh and Israel", CBQ, xxvii, 1965, pp.144-7.

Old Testament Covenant: A Survey of Current Opinions, Oxford, 1972.

Treaty and Covenant: A Study in Form in the Ancient Oriental Documents and the Old Testament, An.Bib. 21, Rome, 1963.

McKane, W.

Prophets and Wise Men, SBT[1] 44, London, 1965.

Proverbs: A New Approach, OTL, London, 1970.

McKay, J.W.

"Exodus XXIII 1-3, 6-8: A Decalogue for the Administration of Justice in the City Gate", VT, xxi, 1971, pp.311-25.

McKeating, H.

"The Development of the Law on Homicide in Ancient Israel", VT, xxv, 1975, pp.46-68.

"Sanctions against Adultery in Ancient Israelite Society, with some Reflections on Methodology in the Study of Old Testament Ethics", JSOT, xi, 1979, pp.57-72.

McKenzie, D.A.

"Judicial Procedure at the Town Gate", VT, xiv, 1964,

pp.100-04.

McKenzie, J.L.

"The Divine Sonship of Israel and the Covenant", CBQ, viii, 1946, pp.320-31.

"The Divine Sonship of Men in the Old Testament", CBQ, vii, 1945, pp.325-39.

"The Elders in the Old Testament", Biblica, xl, 1959, pp.522-40.

Meek, T.J.

Hebrew Origins, New York, revised edition, 1950.

Melugin, R. F.

"The Conventional and the Creative in Isaiah's Judgment Oracles", CBQ, xxxvi, 1974, pp.301-11.

"The Typical versus the Unique among the Hebrew Prophets", Proceedings of the One Hundred Eighth Annual Meeting of the Society of Biblical Literature, ii, 1972, pp.331-41.

Mendenhall, G.E.

"Ancient Oriental and Biblical Law", BA, xvii, 1954, pp.26-46.

"Covenant Forms in Israelite Tradition", BA, xvii, 1954, pp.50-76.

Mendelsohn, I.

"Authority and Law in Canaan-Israel", Authority and Law in the Ancient Orient, JAOS (Supplement 17), 1954, pp.25-33.

"The Canaanite Term for 'Free Proletarian' ", BASOR 83 (October, 1941), pp.36-9.

"On Corvée Labor in Ancient Canaan and Israel", BASOR 167 (October, 1962), pp.31-5.

Legal Aspects of Slavery in Babylonia, Assyria and Palestine: A Comparative Study, Williamsport, 1932.

"Samuel's Denunciation of Kingship in the Light of the Akkadian Documents from Ugarit", BASOR 143 (October, 1956), pp.17-22.

"On Slavery in Alalakh", IEJ, v, 1955, pp.65-72.

"Slavery in the Ancient Near East", BA, ix, 1946, pp.74-88.

Bibliography

<u>Slavery in the Ancient Near East</u>, New York, 1949.

"Slavery in the O.T.", <u>IDB</u>, iv, 1962, pp.383-91.

"State Slavery in Ancient Palestine", <u>BASOR</u> 85
(February, 1942), pp.14-17.
Mettinger, T.N.D.
 <u>Solomonic State Officials: A Study of the Civil
Government Officials of the Israelite Monarchy</u>, Con.Bib.,
<u>Old Testament Series</u> 5, Lund, 1971.
Moriarty, F.L.
 "Prophet and Covenant", <u>Gregorianum</u>, xlvi, 1965,
pp.817-33.
Munn-Rankin, J.M.
 "Diplomacy in Western Asia in the Early Second
Millennium B.C.", <u>Iraq</u>, xviii, 1956, pp.68-110.
Neufeld, E.
 "The Emergence of a Royal-Urban Society in Ancient
Israel", <u>HUCA</u>, xxxi, 1960, pp.31-53.

 "Inalienability of Mobile and Immobile Pledges in the
Laws of the Bible", <u>RIDA</u>[3], ix, 1962, pp.33-44.

 "<u>Ius Redemptionis</u> in Ancient Hebrew Law", <u>RIDA</u>[3],
viii, 1961, pp.29-40.

 "The Prohibitions against Loans at Interest in Ancient
Hebrew Laws", <u>HUCA</u>, xxvi, 1955, pp.355-412.

 "The Rate of Interest and the Text of Nehemiah 5.11",
<u>JQR</u>, N.S., xliv, 1954, pp.194-204.

 "Self-help in Ancient Hebrew Law", <u>RIDA</u>[3], v, 1958,
pp.291-8.

 "Socio-Economic Background of Yöbël and S[e]mitta",
<u>Rivista degli Studi Orientali</u>, xxxiii, 1958, pp.53-124.
Nicholson, E.W.
 <u>Exodus and Sinai in History and Tradition</u>, Oxford, 1973.
Nielsen, K.
 "Das Bild des Gerichts (<u>Rib</u>-Pattern) in Jes. i-xii. Eine
Analyse der Beziehungen zwischen Bildsprache und dem
Anliegen der Verkündigung", <u>VT</u>, xxix, 1979, pp.309-24.

 <u>Yahweh as Prosecutor and Judge</u> (Eng. tr. by Frederick
Cryer, <u>JSOT</u> Supplement Series 9; Sheffield, 1978).
North, R.

"The Biblical Jubilee and Social Reform", Scripture, iv, 1951, pp.323-35.

"Maccabean Sabbath Years", Biblica, xxxiv, 1953, pp.501-15.

Sociology of the Biblical Jubilee, An. Bib. 4, Rome, 1954.

"Yâd in the Shemitta-Law", VT, iv, 1954, pp.196-9.

Noth, M.
Das dritte Buch Mose: Leviticus, ATD 6, Göttingen, 1962 (Eng. tr. by J.E. Anderson, Leviticus: A Commentary, OTL, London, 1965).

Die israelitischen Personennamen im Rahmen der gemeinsemitischen Namengebung, BWANT III, 10, Stuttgart, 1928.

"Das Krongut der israelitischen Könige und seine Verwaltung", ZDPV, 1, 1927, pp.211-44.

Das vierte Buch Mose: Numeri, ATD 7, Göttingen, 1966 (Eng. tr. by J.D. Martin, Numbers: A Commentary, OTL, London, 1968).

Oesterley, W.O.E.
The Book of Proverbs, Westminster Commentaries, London, 1929.

Olivier, J.P.J.
"Schools and Wisdom Literature", JNWSL, iv, 1975, pp.49-60.

Östborn, G.
Tōrā in the Old Testament: A Semantic Study (Eng. tr. from the Swedish original by C. Hentschel, Lund, 1945).

Oyen, H. van
Ethik des Alten Testaments, Gütersloh, 1967.

Pedersen, J.
Israel: Its Life and Culture, i-ii, London and Copenhagen, 1926 (Eng. tr. from the Danish original by A. Møller, Copenhagen, 1920).

Perlitt, L.
Bundestheologie im Alten Testament, WMANT 36, Neukirchen, 1969.

Phillips, A.
Ancient Israel's Criminal Law: A New Approach to the Decalogue, Oxford, 1970.

"The Case of the Woodgatherer Reconsidered", VT, xix, 1969, pp.125-8.

"The Interpretation of 2 Samuel xii 5-6", VT, xvi, 1966, pp.242-4.

Ploeg, J. van der
"Les Anciens dans l'Ancien Testament", Lex Tua Veritas (H. Junker Festschrift), eds. H. Gross and F. Mussner, Trier, 1961, pp.175-91.

"Les chefs du peuple d'Israël et leurs titres", RB, lvii, 1950, pp.40-61.

"Les Pauvres d'Israël et leur piété", OTS, vii, 1950, pp. 236-70.

"Studies in Hebrew Law IV", CBQ, xiii, 1951, pp.164-71.

Porteous, N.W.
"The Basis of the Ethical Teaching of the Prophets", Studies in Old Testament Prophecy, ed. H.H. Rowley, Edinburgh, 1950, pp.143-56.

Procksch, O.
Jesaia I, KAT IX, Leipzig, 1930.

Rabinowitz, J.J.
"A Biblical Parallel to a Legal Formula from Ugarit", VT, viii, 1958, p.95.

Rad, G. von
Das erste Buch Mose: Genesis, ATD 2-4, Göttingen, 1949-53 (Eng. tr. by J.H. Marks, Genesis: A Commentary, OTL, London, 1961; revised edition, 1972).

Das fünfte Buch Mose: Deuteronomium, ATD 8, Göttingen, 1964 (Eng. tr. by Dorothea Barton, Deuteronomy: A Commentary, OTL, London, 1966).

Theologie des Alten Testaments, i, München, 1957 (Eng. tr. by D.M.G. Stalker, Old Testament Theology, i, Edinburgh, 1962); Theologie des Alten Testaments, ii, München, 1960 (Eng. tr. by D.M.G. Stalker, Old Testament Theology, ii, Edinburgh, 1965).

Weisheit in Israel, Neukirchen, 1970 (Eng. tr. by J.D. Martin, Wisdom in Israel, London, 1972).

Rainey, A.F.
"Administration in Ugarit and the Samaria Ostraca", IEJ, xii, 1962, pp.62-3.

"The Kingdom of Ugarit", BA, xxviii, 1965, pp.102-25.

"The Samaria Ostraca in the Light of Fresh Evidence", PEQ, xcix, 1967, pp.32-41.
Rapaport, I.
    "The Origins of Hebrew Law", PEQ, lxxiii, 1941, pp.158-67.
Robinson, H. Wheeler
    "The Council of Yahweh", JTS, xlv, 1944, pp.151-7.
Robinson, T.H.
    "Higher Criticism and the Prophetic Literature", Exp.T., l, 1938-9, pp.198-202.

    Prophecy and the Prophets in Ancient Israel, London, 1923.
Rudolph, W.
    Esra und Nehemia, HAT, I, 20, Tübingen, 1949.
Sarna, N.
    "Zedekiah's Emancipation of Slaves and the Sabbatical Year", Orient and Occident (C.H. Gordon Festschrift), ed. H.A. Hoffner, Alter Orient und Altes Testament 22, 1973, pp.143-9.
Schlisske, W.
    Gottessöhne und Gottessohn im Alten Testament, BWANT V, 17, Stuttgart, 1973.
Schmid, H.H.
    "Amos. Zur Frage nach der 'geistigen Heimat' des Propheten", WuD, N.F., x, 1969, pp.85-103.
Schwarz, G.
    "'Begünstige nicht...'? (Leviticus 19, 15b)", Bib. Zeit., N.F., xix, 1975, p.100.
Scott, R.B.Y.
    "The Book of Isaiah, Chapters 1-39", IB, v, 1956, pp.151-381.

    "The Literary Structure of Isaiah's Oracles", Studies in Old Testament Prophecy, ed. H.H. Rowley, Edinburgh, 1950, pp.175-86.

    Proverbs. Ecclesiastes, Anchor Bible, New York, 1965.

    "Solomon and the Beginnings of Wisdom in Israel", VTS, iii, 1955, pp. 262-79.

    The Way of Wisdom, New York, 1971.
Seebass, H.
    "Der Fall Naboth in 1 Reg. XXI", VT, xxiv, 1974, pp. 474-88.

Bibliography

Skehan, P.W.
"The Structure of the Song of Moses in Deuteronomy (Deut. 32:1-43)", CBQ, xiii, 1951, pp.153-63.

Skinner, J.
The Book of the Prophet Isaiah I-XXXIX, Cambridge, 1896.

Sklba, R.J.
"The Redeemer of Israel", CBQ, xxxiv, 1972, pp.1-18.

Snaith, N.H.
"The Daughters of Zelophehad", VT, xvi, 1966, pp.124-7.

Speiser, E.A.
"'Coming' and 'Going' at the 'City' Gate", BASOR 144 (December, 1956), pp.20-3.

Genesis, Anchor Bible, New York, 1964.

"New Kirkuk Documents Relating to Security Transactions", JAOS, lii, 1932, pp.350-67.

Steele, F.R.
Nuzi Real Estate Transactions, American Oriental Society 25, New Haven, 1943.

Stein, S.
"The Laws on Interest in the Old Testament", JTS, N.S., iv, 1953, pp.161-70.

Talmon, S.
"The New Hebrew Letter from the Seventh Century B.C. in Historical Perspective", BASOR 176 (December, 1964), pp.29-38.

Terrien, S.
"Amos and Wisdom", Israel's Prophetic Heritage, eds. B.W. Anderson and W. Harrelson, London, 1962, pp.108-15.

Thompson, J.A.
"The Near Eastern Suzerain-Vassal Concept in the Religion of Israel", JRH, iii, 1964, pp.1-19.

Tucker, G.M.
"The Legal Background of Genesis 23", JBL, lxxxv, 1966, pp.77-84.

"Witnesses and 'Dates' in Israelite Contracts", CBQ, xxviii, 1966, pp.42-5.

de Vaux, R.
Les Institutions de l'Ancien Testament, Paris, two volumes, 1958-60 (Eng. tr. by J. McHugh, Ancient Israel: Its Life and Institutions, London, 1961).

Victor, P.

"A Note on חק in the Old Testament", <u>VT</u>, xvi, 1966, pp.358-61.

Vollmer, J.
<u>Geschichtliche Rückblicke und Motive in der Prophetie des Amos, Hosea und Jesaja</u>, <u>BZAW</u> 119, Berlin, 1971.

Vriezen, T.C.
"Essentials of the Theology of Isaiah", <u>Israel's Prophetic Heritage</u>, eds. B.W. Anderson and W. Harrelson, London, 1962, pp.128-46.

Wacholder, B.Z.
"The Calendar of Sabbatical Cycles during the Second Temple and the Early Rabbinic Period", <u>HUCA</u>, xliv, 1973, pp.153-96.

von Waldow, H.E.
"Social Responsibility and Social Structure in Early Israel", <u>CBQ</u>, xxxii, 1970, pp.182-204.

<u>Der traditionsgeschichtliche Hintergrund der prophetischen Gerichtsreden</u>, <u>BZAW</u> 85, Berlin, 1963.

Wanke, G.
" אוי und הוי", <u>ZAW</u>, lxxviii, 1966, pp.215-8.

Weber, M.
<u>Gesammelte Aufsätze zur Religionssoziologie III, Das antike Judentum</u>, Tübingen, 1921 (Eng. tr. and edited by H.H. Gerth and D. Martindale, <u>Ancient Judaism</u>, Glencoe, 1952).

Weinfeld, M.
"Traces of Assyrian Treaty Formulae in Deuteronomy", <u>Biblica</u>, xlvi, 1965, pp.417-27.

Weingreen, J.
"The Case of the Daughters of Zelophchad", <u>VT</u>, xvi, 1966, pp.518-22.

"The Case of the Woodgatherer (Numbers XV 32-36)", <u>VT</u>, xvi, 1966, pp.361-4.

"The Rebellion of Absalom", <u>VT</u>, xix, 1969, pp.263-6.

Wellhausen, J.
<u>Geschichte Israels</u>, i, Marburg, 1878; second edition, <u>Prolegomena zur Geschichte Israels</u>, Berlin, 1883 (Eng. tr. of this second edition by J.S. Black and A. Menzies, <u>Prolegomena to the History of Israel</u>, Edinburgh, 1885).

Welten, P.
"Naboths Weinberg (1 Könige 21)", <u>EvTh</u>, xxxiii, 1973, pp.

18-32.

Westbrook, R.
"Jubilee Laws", ILR, vi, 1971, pp.209-26.

Westermann, C.
Grundformen prophetischer Rede, München, 1960 (Eng. tr. by Hugh Clayton White, Basic Forms of Prophetic Speech, London, 1967).

Whedbee, J.W.
Isaiah and Wisdom, Nashville - New York, 1971.

Whitehouse, O.C.
Isaiah I-XXXIX, Cent.B., London, 1905.

Whitelam, K.W.
The Just King: Monarchial Judicial Authority in Ancient Israel, JSOT Supplement Series 12; Sheffield, 1979.

Whitley, C.F.
The Prophetic Achievement, London, 1963.

Whybray, R.N.
The Intellectual Tradition in the Old Testament, BZAW 135, Berlin, 1974.

Wisdom in Proverbs, SBT[1] 45, London, 1965.

Wildberger, H.
"Israel und sein Land", EvTh, xvi, 1956, pp.404-22.

Jesaja, BKAT X/1, Neukirchen, 1972.

Williams, J.G.
"The Alas-Oracles of the Eighth Century Prophets", HUCA, xxxviii, 1967, pp.75-91.

Willis, J.T.
"The Genre of Isaiah 5:1-7", JBL, xcvi, 1977, pp.337-62.

Wiseman, D.J.
The Alalakh Tablets, London, 1953.

"The Vassal-Treaties of Esarhaddon", Iraq, xx, 1958, pp. 1-99.

Wolf, C.U.
"Traces of Primitive Democracy in Ancient Israel", JNES, vi, 1947, pp.98-108.

Wolff, H.W.
Amos' geistige Heimat, WMANT 18, Neukirchen, 1964 (Eng. tr. by F.R. McCurley, Amos the Prophet. The Man and his Background, Philadelphia, 1973).

Joel und Amos, BKAT XIV/2, Neukirchen, 1969 (Eng. tr. by W. Janzen, S. Dean McBride, Jr., and C.A. Muenchow,

Joel and Amos, Philadelphia, 1977).

Wright, G.E.
"The Book of Deuteronomy", IB, ii, 1953, pp.311-537.

"The Faith of Israel", IB, i, 1952, pp.349-89.

"The Lawsuit of God: A Form-Critical Study of Deuteronomy 32", *Israel's Prophetic Heritage*, eds. B.W. Anderson and W. Harrelson, London, 1962, pp.26-67.

The Old Testament against its Environment, SBT[1] 2, London, 1950.

"The Terminology of Old Testament Religion and its Significance", JNES, i, 1942, pp.404-14.

Würthwein, E.
"Amos-Studien", ZAW, lxii, 1950, pp.10-52.

"Der Ursprung der prophetischen Gerichtsrede", ZThK, xlix, 1952, pp.1-16.

Yadin, Y.
"Ancient Judaean Weights and the Date of the Samaria Ostraca", *Scripta Hierosolymitana*, viii, 1961, pp.9-25.

"Recipients or Owners: A Note on the Samaria Ostraca", IEJ, ix, 1959, pp.184-7.

Zimmerli, W.
Das Gesetz und die Propheten: Zum Verständnis des Alten Testamentes, Göttingen, 1963 (Eng. tr. by R.E. Clements, The Law and the Prophets: A Study of the Meaning of the Old Testament, Oxford, 1965).

INDEX OF SUBJECTS

INDEX OF AUTHORS

INDEX OF BIBLICAL REFERENCES

Index of Biblical References

5:22-4	91	**Jeremiah**	
5:23	93f.,107f.,117	2:12	54
5:24	38	2:22	91
6:1ff.	30,57	3:19	46
6:3	13	4:28	45
6:9	62	5:22	82
6:10	30,134	6:18f.	55
7:3ff.	33	8:7	49
8:6,11f.	134	18:18	35,125
8:9f.	33	23:18ff.	57
9:8-20	23	26:1ff.	52f.
10:1	82	26:10ff.	96
10:1ff.	27,82	26:11	53,55f.
10:1-4	81,91,102,111,142	32:6ff.	70
10:4a	81	34	71,137
10:5ff.	33	34:8,15,17	137
10:15	31	49:11	103
19:1ff.	33		
22:15	77	**Lamentations**	
23:4	40	5:3	147
28:7-13,14-22	23		
28:14ff.	33	**Ezekiel**	
28:23ff.	33,125	18:8	68
28:23-9	31	22:7	103
29:14	35	22:12	67,93
29:15f.	33	46:16-18	139
30:1,9	46		
30:1ff.	33	**Daniel**	
30:15-17	23	10:20	144
31:1ff.	33		
31:2	35	**Hosea**	
33:22	82	1:9	134
41:1	55	5:1	143
44:23	44	5:1f.	95
48:10	91	6:7	20
49:1	55	7:13	48
49:13	44	8:1	20
49:21	40	9:12	40
51:18	40	11:1	46
52:3ff.	143		
59:17-20	143	**Joel**	
61:1-4	139	4:12	52
61:8	143		

F